GRAMPIAN

Edited by Kelly Oliver

First published in Great Britain in 2003 by
YOUNG WRITERS
Remus House,
Coltsfoot Drive,
Peterborough, PE2 9JX
Telephone (01733) 890066

SB ISBN 1 84460 302 4

FOREWORD

Young Writers was established in 1991 as a foundation for promoting the reading and writing of poetry amongst children and young adults. Today it continues this quest and proceeds to nurture and guide the writing talents of today's youth.

From this year's competition Young Writers is proud to present a showcase of the best poetic talent from across the UK. Each hand-picked poem has been carefully chosen from over 66,000 'Hullabaloo!' entries to be published in this, our eleventh primary school series.

This year in particular we have been wholeheartedly impressed with the quality of entries received. The thought, effort, imagination and hard work put into each poem impressed us all and once again the task of editing was a difficult but enjoyable experience.

We hope you are as pleased as we are with the final selection and that you and your family will continue to be entertained with *Hullabaloo! Grampian* for many years to come.

CONTENTS

Robert Murray (10) 1

Alehousewells Primary School, Inverurie

Ann Taylor (11) 1
Ryan Anderson & Liam Thom (10) 2
Scott Davis (11) 3
Stuart Miller (11) 4
Kirsty Donald (11) 5
Kirsty Wilson (11) 6
Sarah Gall (11) 6
Stephanie Fraser (11) 7
Natalie Beaton & Pamela Cheyne (11) 8

Banff Primary School, Banff

Steven Watson (8) 9
Lisa Killah (9) 9
Scott Smith (11) 10
Fiona Faye Christie (7) 10
Struan Robertson (11) 11
Aaron Evans (11) 12
Stephanie Grant (11) 13
Leigh Killah (11) 14
Kieren Macphee (11) 14
Meghan Coady (11) 15
Laura Barr (11) 16
Demi Mair (11) 17
Tom Seed 17
Lauren Clarke (8) 18
Joseph Jeffrey (8) 18
Steven MacDonald (8) 19
Rebecca Anderson (9) 19
Stacey Murphy (8) 20
Rachael A Hay (10) 20
Siobhan McAllister (8) 21
Connon Mackenzie (10) 21
Adele Buchan (8) 22

Andrew Walker (10) 23
Kristofer Alexander (10) 23
Jamie Davies (11) 24
Kieran MacGregor (8) 24
Iain McKean (10) 25
Nicola Cook (10) 25
Andrew Mathieson (10) 26
Stuart Murray (10) 27
Catherine Knowlson (10) 27
Faye Smith (10) 28
Michael McGregor (10) 28
Jon Watson (10) 29
Keith Rennie (10) 29
Andrew Davidson (10) 30
Jennifer Gordon (10) 30
Scott Shearer (8) 31
Kieran Alexander (9) 31
Kerr Baptie (8) 32
Shannan Gallon (8) 32
Stephanie Skinner (11) 33
Samantha Morrison (11) 33
Daniel Ewen (11) 34
Graeme Martin (8) 34
Patrick Fisher (10) 35
John Sloan (8) 35
Ashleigh Strain (10) 36
Nicole Knott (8) 36
Emma-Louise Reid (11) 37
Milo Mole (8) 37
Mark Cole (10) 38
Sarah Barr (8) 38
Ryan Buchan (10) 39
Scott Mathieson (8) 39
Amy Gatt (8) 40
Cameron McAllister (8) 40
Kieran Morrison (10) 41
James Mackintosh (10) 41
Martin Mitchell (12) 42

Ashley Hall (11) 43
Jordon Reid (8) 43
Laurence Woods (11) 44
Amy Yorkston (10) 44
Vicky Noble (11) 45
Daniel Thomson (10) 45
Sophie Pellett (10) 46
Gavin Watt (10) 47
Jonathon Gatt (10) 47
Jason Smith (10) 48
Christopher Davidson (11) 48
Ross Bligdon (10) 49
Kelly-Anne Innes (10) 49
Peter Day (10) 50
Paul Stuart (10) 50
Rosemary Coles (10) 51
Darryl Duncan (11) 51
Jenna Killoh (11) 52
Martyn Shand (11) 52
Sarah Murray (11) 53
Lucy Montrose (11) 54
Michaela Ure (8) 54
Jamie Wilson (11) 55
Allan Cook (8) 55
Emma Pantel (8) 56

Clatt Primary School, Huntly
Neil Anderson (9) 56
Michelle Connon (7) 56
Francesca Walsh (9) 57
Andrew Chalmers (10) 57
John Connon (10) 57

Crombie Primary School, Westhill
Jessica Wright (10) 58
Lisa McCarrol (10) 58
Stuart McMaster (10) 59
Danielle Allan (10) 60

Leanne Wilson (10) 60
Jennifer Park (10) 61
Lynsey Irvine (10) 61
Faye Cumming (10) 62
Kathryn Hunter (10) 63
Sophie Svensen (10) 64
Robyn Hay (10) 64
Kerri Hendry (10) 65
Jordan Connell (10) 65
Clara-Jane Irvine (10) 66
Iain Smith (10) 67
Hannah Svensen (10) 68
Leila Smithers (10) 68
Matthew Hinton (10) 69
Ruth McGlashan (9) 69
Daniel Ferguson (10) 70
Julia Bryce (10) 71
Mairi Farquharson (10) 72
Laura Watson (10) 72
Karin Moir (10) 73
Chris Robertson (10) 73
Roanna Scott (10) 74
Abbey Sproul (10) 74
Emma Brewer (10) 75
Kyle Cowin (10) 75
Shaun Johnson (10) 76
Abbie Forsyth (10) 76
Bethany Lawson (9) 77
Daniel Rodgers (10) 77
Gemma Reid (10) 78
Rachael Nicol (10) 78
Robert Elrick (10) 79
Amy McTavish (10) 79
Lewis Murchie (10) 80
Fraser Irvine (10) 80
Josephine Alexander (10) 81
Michael Watson (10) 81
Rebecca Paterson (11) 82

Reece Manson (10) 82
Scott Moir (10) 83
Gregor Morrice (10) 83
Nicole Beedie (10) 84
Ewan Diack (11) 84
Caroline Will (10) 85
Verity Clark (10) 85
Hayley Brown (10) 85
Andrew Coates (10) 86

Culter Primary School, Peterculter
Megan Quinn (10) 86
Joanne Murphy (10) 87
Sean McFarlane (10) 87
Jorja Anderson (10) 88
William McKay (11) 88
Liam Shaw (11) 89
Sandra Stewart (10) 89
Dailin Hope (10) 90
Kayleigh Fraser (10) 90
Kirsty Donaldson (10) 91
Jodie Selfridge (10) 91
Sacha Christie (10) 92
Keelan Pirie (10) 92
Carla England (11) 93
Jamie Stroud (10) 93
Jennifer Robb (10) 94
Mark Smith (10) 94
Nikki Cunningham (10) 95
Natalie Robb (10) 95
Euan Ferguson (10) 96
Leanne Christie (10) 97
Matthew Kidd (11) 98
Somhairle Cruickshank (10) 99
Ewan McRae (10) 100
Nicole Ross (10) 101
Jordan Sparrow (10) 102

East End Primary School, Elgin

Sarah Mills (10) 103
Claire Grant (10) 103
Duncan Innes (10) 104
Ian Thomson (10) 104
Ashleigh Grant (10) 105
Calum Leiper (10) 105
Lauren Ford (10) 106
Stewart McLaren (10) 106
Hannah Scott (10) 107
Georgia Stewart (11) 107
Stacey Jackson (10) 108
Callum Watson (10) 108
Joe Williams (11) 109
Zara-Ann McKenzie (11) 109
Steven Lyons (11) 110
Allan Slapp (10) 110
Steven Webster (10) 111
Staci Smith (10) 111
Lauren Hambly (11) 112
Gemma-Louise Taylor (11) 112
Claire Sutherland (12) 113
Michael Paterson (11) 113
Andrew Jackson (12) 114
Kenneth Greaves (11) 114
Ross Archibald (11) 115
Jamie-Ann Docherty (11) 115
Liam Archibald (11) 116

Foveran Primary School, Foveran

Stephanie Asher (10) 116
Sarah Buchan & Norman Campbell (11) 117
Johnathan Kain (9) 117
Ryan Bennett (10) 118
Kathryn Cruickshank (10) 118
Nicola Buchan (9) 119
Stephen Nightingale (9) 119
Iona McLeod (10) 120

Fyvie Primary School, Turriff
Harry Reeder (9) 120
Kirsten Gall (10) 121
Fiona Crawford (9) 121
Emily England (8) 122
Mary Heaton (10) 122
Arran Donald (11) 123
Martyn Black (11) 123
Sophie McWilliam (11) 124
Philip Woodward (9) 124
Marion Fisher (10) 125
Robbie Faquhar (9) 125
Lyndsay Mackie (10) 126
William Wilson (11) 126
Caroline Esslemont (10) 127
Aidan Hutcheon (9) 127
Holly Johnston (11) 128
Monica Crawford (9) 128
Gill Christie (11) 129
Ben Bardsley (8) 129
Gemma Forbes (11) 130
Gavin Taylor (11) 130
Alex Pithie (11) 131
Harry Hanson (11) 131
Faye Mailley (11) 132
Rebecca Conn (11) 133
Sam Wilson (9) 134
Sarah Davidson (11) 134
Emily Horn (11) 135
Peter Davies (9) 135
Janine Gall (11) 136
Sheila Edwards (11) 136
Amy Singer (10) 137

Insch Primary School, Insch
Rebekah Wright (12) 137
Andrew McNamee (11) 138
Lee Gillies (11) 138

Jennifer Simpson (11) 139
Lucy Rowe (11) 140
Eilidh Leask (11) 141
Jessica Norrie (12) 142
Abby Kelman (11) 143
Nicola Farquhar (11) 144
Tania Moir (11) 145

Kennethmont School, Huntly
Calum Howard (11) 146
Darryl McLaughlin (11) 146
Rhuaraidh Docherty (11) 147
Fiona Webster (9) 147
Sean Webb (11) 148
Liam Paterson (10) 148
Ryan Dawson (10) 149
Katy Campbell (10) 150
Lorna Gordon (9) 150
Ashley Cruickshank (10) 151
Kirsten Docherty (10) 151
Amy Grant (11) 152
Claire Drysdale (9) 152
Emily Phillips (10) 152

Mintlaw Primary School, Peterhead
Andrew Mair (8) 153
Ellen Bain (8) 153
Craig Hutcheon (8) 153
Lisa Sutherland (8) 154
Dale Nicoll (8) 154
Karen Hayward (8) 154
Michael Howie (9) 155
Alistair McKay (8) 155
Billie-Jo Monaghan (8) 156

Port Elphinstone Primary School, Inverurie
Matthew Banks (10) 156
Joshua Michie (9) 157

Kareen Webster (9) 157
Callum Murray (9) 158
Vikki Mennie (9) 158
Laura Mackie (9) 159
David Ferguson (9) 159
Frazer Christie (10) 160
Lisa Finnigan (9) 160

St Andrew's Primary School, Fraserburgh
Liam Noble (8) 161
Sarah-Marie Gault (8) 161
Kirsty Alexander (8) 162
Joshua Masson (8) 162
Stephen Watt (8) 163
Hayley McIntosh (8) 163
Alistair Eddie (9) 164
Calum MacLeod (8) 164
Steven Buchan (8) 165
Emma May (8) 165
Christopher Mackie (8) 166
Sarah-Jane Bisset (8) 166
Ross West (8) 167
Neil Holland (8) 167

St Gerardine Primary School, Lossiemouth
Austin Lennon (11) 168
Craig Smith (10) 168
Sean McEneany (9) 169
Ruth Corps (10) 169
Charlotte Fairminer (11) 170
Claire Matthews (11) 170
Emily Alldritt (10) 171
Ewan Thomson (11) 171
Chloe McKay (10) 172
Hannah Gordon (11) 173
Sean Cross (11) 173
Michael McLeod (10) 174
Ross Diack (11) 174

Christopher Jennings (11) 175
Charlotte Wilson (10) 175
Gary Campbell (11) 176
Malcolm Hendry (10) 176
Kirsty Smith (10) 177
Kirsteen Richardson (11) 177
Rhuraidh Garness (11) 178
Daniel Baker (11) 178
Zara Petrie (11) 179
Emily Stewart (10) 179
Alexander Florence (11) 180
Frazer McKechnie (11) 180
Culum Graham (10) 181
Michael Spring (11) 181
William Clunas (11) 182
Laurie Gill (10) 182
Amy McLeod (11) 183
Chelsea Logan (10) 183
Joseph Fleetwood (11) 183
Chelsea Cruickshank (11) 184

St Sylvester's Primary School, Elgin

Jordan Stuart (10) 184
Anthony Brannigan (9) 185
Louise Masson (10) 185
Stephanie Parry (10) 186
Jodie Jones (10) 186
Melissa Grant (10) 187
Katrina Andrews (9) 187
Heather Burns (11) 188
Amber Hayward (10) 188
Agnes Neal (10) 188
Barry James Moir (10) 189
Kerry Hesten (10) 189

St Thomas' RC Primary School, Keith

Claire Morrison (11) 190
Gary Mitchell (11) 190

Craig Sims (10) 191
Laura Bowie (9) 191
Robert Main (11) 192
Rachel McKay (11) 192
Sophie Webster (11) 193
Gary Smith (11) 193
Jaqui Stewart (9) 194

Seafield Primary School, Elgin

Kyle Lear (8) 194
Diane Mackay (10) 195
Jenna McKidd & Kelly Noble (10) 195
Callum Ord (11) 196
Katie McKerrell & Sally Lapington (9) 196
Kyle Stewart & Shaun Grant (11) 197
Jonathan Roe & Cameron Robertson (10) 197
Lynsey Blair (10) 198
Alice Stewart (8) 198
Hayleigh Stephenson (10) 199
Sean MacDonald (8) 199
Kelly Grieve (11) 200
Ebony Grant (7) 200
Brian Walker (10) 201
Alannah Russell (7) 201
Danny Stuart (11) 202
Sam Watts (8) 202
Becky Lapington (10) 203
Connor Kelman (7) 203
Jorden Davies (10) 204
Connor Sutherland (8) 204
Melissa McKerrell (11) 205
Euan Slater (7) 205
Natalie Stephen (11) 206
Rhiannon McAllister (8) 206
Caasi McCrindle (11) 207
Kayleigh Ritchie (8) 207
Leanne Prescott (11) 208
Brittany Hulley (7) 208

Paul McMillan (10)	209
Kristina Nightingale (10)	209
Johnathon Beveridge (11)	210
Laura McCrindle (10)	210
Joe Kelman (10)	211
Kirsty Wilkie (10)	211
Caitlin Innes (11)	212
Garey Steele (11)	213
Laura Morrison (10)	213
Linzi Harvey (11)	214
Barrie Thompson (11)	214
Angela Dean (9)	215
Yasmin Anderson (11)	215
Chloe Walker (11)	216
Jamie Wiseman (11)	216
Philip Garioch (12)	216
Ryan O'Shane (11)	217
Tanya Ross (11)	217
Fiona Wilkie (12)	217
Steven Chadwick (11)	218
Rebecca Cameron (11)	218
Natasha Macdonald (11)	219
Claire Forbes (11)	219
Cassie McCutcheon (11)	220
Samantha Mathieson (11)	220
Ashley Barnes (10)	221
Kirsty Farquhar (10)	221
Beth Little (10)	222
Ross Hudson (11)	222
Vicki Smedley (11)	223
Hannah Pacey (11)	223
Heather Penman (11)	224
Nathan Mitchell (11)	225
Daniel Clark (9)	226
Jason Brownless (11)	226
Peta Greer (10)	227
Lee Stewart (11)	227
Rhian Fairgrieve (9)	228

Joshua Bawden (11) 228
Stephanie Grieve (9) 229
Samira Kabbani (10) 229
Alastair Milligan (10) 230
Laura Wilson (10) 231
Jessica Knox (10) 232
Leanne Kelly (10) 232
Lucy McShane (9) 233
Scott McKee (10) 233
Charlie Welsh (9) 234
Dean Webster (10) 234
Lauren Wimble (9) 235
Grant Fletcher (10) 235
Demi Tewnion (9) 236
Jamie Neil (10) 236
Christina Marshall (9) 237
Josie Scott (9) 237
Chantelle Ord (9) 238
Sarah Watts (9) 238
Chloe Baxter (8) 239
Taran Read (9) 239
Calum Davies (9) 240
Joanna O'Neill (9) 241
Lucy Redfern (9) 242
Kieran Butcher (8) 243
Sam Sherwin (9) 243
Kaylie McRae (9) 244
Andrew McKenzie (9) 244
Megan McQueen (8) 245
Scott McGarrie (9) 245
David Manson (9) 246
Steven Curran (9) 246

Slains Primary School, Ellon
Laura Penny (12) 247
Zoe Sinclair (10) 248

Westhill Primary School, Westhill

Lisa M Irvine (12)	248
Jamie McNaughton (11)	249
Emily Pettitt (11)	249
Harry Burness (11)	250
Lewis Illingworth (11)	250
Emma Rae (11)	251
Aidan Fleming (11)	251
Victoria Willan (10)	252
Kelsey Longmuir (11)	252
Steven Repper (11)	253
Callum Ogston (11) & Ewan Mackay (12)	253
Jenna Goff (11)	254
Michael MacDonald (11)	255
Ailsa Mullins (11)	256
Euan Dodds (9)	256
Scott Milne (9)	257
Katie Jones (11)	257
Johanna Goldie (9)	258
Michael Ridley (11)	258
Morag Will (11)	259
Fraser Clarke & David Sutherland (11)	259
Kayleigh Milne (11)	260
Arron Sturrock & Oran Lasocki (11)	260

The Poems

A Plane

A good way to travel is on a plane,
On top of the clouds,
On top of the rain.

A good way to travel is on a plane,
Sometimes all night,
Sometimes all day.

A good way to travel is on a plane,
Sitting or sleeping
Or playing a game.

Robert Murray (10)

Eternity

I am sad, I am bored,
Every morning I reflect a tearful, miserable face.
I wish I could see something exciting,
Even just a new face.
I am trapped,
My owner sits all alone,
I am a mirror who faces down,
She never lets anyone touch me.
I am sad, I am bored,
It looks like it will stay this way,
For all eternity.

Ann Taylor (11)
Alehousewells Primary School, Inverurie

A Sick Poem

'My head is spinning
My eyes are sore
My throat is throbbing
I feel very poor

My nose is runny
My ears are aching
My chest is so hot
I feel it is baking

My stomach is burning
My hips are dead
My legs feel like jelly
Can I please stay in bed?'

'No you cannot
You look pretty well
Remember if you're lying
You'll go straight to *Hell!'*

'So can I . . .'

'No!'

Ryan Anderson & Liam Thom (10)
Alehousewells Primary School, Inverurie

MIRROR

I am as big as a tote tray,
My rim is narrow, pencil-like.
My owners adore me,
Every day my people gaze into me,
I live in the kitchen, where, on the wall, I hang,
Staring at a rusty old oven.

They fiddle with their hair,
Put on make-up and rub on their spot cream.

I show them their real reflections
And they are always pleased that *I do not lie* to them.
When the central heating is on or they are cooking,
I start to steam up,
Everything becomes blurry to me.
Then their teenage son will come along
And write stuff on me when I'm steamed up.
I always know it's him because he's always dressed
In the same dark clothes that I can only just see through the steam.

He writes swear words on me, rude things that only the most
Heartless person could write on a mirror.
He always gets caught though.
His parents will always wipe the words and steam off me,
I can see again.

When darkness strikes, I'm all alone, no one around me.
I dream bad dreams, I remember the days
When I was sitting on a shelf, in a very dark box.
I was scared, but then finally I was taken off the shelf
And opened up after a *long* time.
I was free,
I, at long last, had been taken out of the box
And hung up on a wall, I had owners.

Scott Davis (11)
Alehousewells Primary School, Inverurie

FLANNAN ISLE

Three men sailed, only they knew where
Until they came to an isle there
They anchored the ship and left it be
They counted crows, they saw three

As time passed they climbed and climbed
But no end they seemed to find
Until at last but all too soon
They came to the top, they had to swoon

Behind the door, an untouched meal
As well as an old, used fishing creel
Although they searched high and low
There was no evidence on show

And so they left the dreaded house
They heard nothing, not even a mouse
Three men alive on Flannan Isle
Who thought it wasn't worth the while.

Stuart Miller (11)
Alehousewells Primary School, Inverurie

FLANNAN ISLE

From far across the land, three men sailed
To find the story that had been wailed.
They saw queer, blackbirds keeping watch,
As if guarding the lighthouse on the rock.

But when they landed upon the island,
No noise was heard, only silence.
The men were scared, but plucked up courage
And up the rocks they quickly hurried.

They entered the lighthouse with silent steps,
The place was clean, the floor neatly swept.
There was a table with a checked table spread
And meat and cheese and biscuit and bread.

They searched the building high and low
And over the island to and fro.
Of the men's fate they found no trace,
Of any kind in any place.

They seemed to stand for an endless while,
Thinking about the mystery of Flannan Isle,
But still no dreaded words were said
About the men that were thought on dead.

Kirsty Donald (11)
Alehousewells Primary School, Inverurie

Drizzling Rain

Rain, falling gently,
Sinking to the ground,
Like mice whispering softly,
Like soft bird feathers,
Swooping through the night.
Her fingers are
Twinkling,
Her toes are
Waving.
Always blinking
With her eyes,
Making tears drizzle by.
So sweet and gentle,
The drizzling rain.

Kirsty Wilson (11)
Alehousewells Primary School, Inverurie

Cats

Cats are cute,
Cats are fluffy,
Some are mute,
I think they are puffy.

Cats are fat,
My one is flat,
He was run over,
I think by a Rover.

Sarah Gall (11)
Alehousewells Primary School, Inverurie

My New Boyfriend!

I came home from school,
Apparently dreamy.
My mum glanced at me and said,
'Who is he?'

I told her I had no idea what she meant,
(While I was reading the love note he sent!)

I started to make tea,
Bangers and mash!
Then went to watch some fab movie scenes,
My mum suddenly screamed,
I saw what was wrong.

'Mum, you told me to spill the beans!'

Stephanie Fraser (11)
Alehousewells Primary School, Inverurie

I'M ILL

My head is thumping,
My eyes are sore,
My heart is jumping,
Need I say more?

My stomach is churning,
My joints all creak,
My hips are burning,
It started this week!

My legs are throbbing,
My knees are aching,
I feel like sobbing,
My toes are baking.

Mum, do I have to go to school?

Natalie Beaton & Pamela Cheyne (11)
Alehousewells Primary School, Inverurie

Little Larry And Huge Harry

Larry is little
Harry is huge
And both of them like to groove.

Larry's face is pointed
Harry's face is round
If they're not careful they will end up
In the dog pound

Larry's hair is soft and smooth
Harry's hair is long and tangled
I wonder
How it gets so scruffy?

Larry's tail is short and stubby
Harry's tail is long and large
And he wants a wife called Marge.

Steven Watson (8)
Banff Primary School, Banff

Planets

P lanets
L arge and small
A mazing
N ine planets
E xciting
T winkling
S pace.

Lisa Killah (9)
Banff Primary School, Banff

I'm An Evacuee

I'm an evacuee,
I've just been evacuated,
Where am I going?

I have been re-homed now,
It's time for me to go to bed,
In my bed, I can't sleep
Because I think of all the children
That were crying and saying goodbye
To family and friends.

Six years later I got sent home,
To find my house had been bombed,
All of my belongings are destroyed,
So what do I do now?

Scott Smith (11)
Banff Primary School, Banff

Horses In Showing

Hooves hitting
Over the jumps
Riders sitting high
Excitement in the sky
Off comes their tack and on goes the rugs
The showers collect their prizes
And off they go home.

Fiona Faye Christie (7)
Banff Primary School, Banff

I Miss Home

I'm an evacuee
And I'm not very happy
I'm not very bad
But I miss Mum and Dad
I just want to go home

I'm an evacuee
And I'm not very happy
I hate Germany
The billeting officer is a granny
I just want to go home

I'm an evacuee
And I'm not very happy
The lady looking at me is a bat
And she smells like a rat
I just want to go home

I'm an evacuee
And I'm not very happy
I'm not very moody
I just want some food in me
I just want to go home.

Struan Robertson (11)
Banff Primary School, Banff

WORLD WAR II

I'm on the train
Watching the rain

The train stops
The door opens

I get out
People shout

I'm the last to go
In the row

I see the lady I want
But she's gone

I have to stay
With Mrs Way

She's nice
She smells of spice

Why did Hitler go
And bomb my home?

Aaron Evans (11)
Banff Primary School, Banff

WORLD WAR II

Children are crying
People are dying
Hitler was lying

Boom, bang!

Today is the day when I say goodbye to Mum and Dad
It's all very sad
I am away to a new home
I am all alone!

Boom, bang!

I step off the train, I have a sore tummy
I wish I had my mummy
A tall, plump, kind woman came over to me
'I'll take her and give her some tea.'

Boom, bang!

When will it stop?
Tomorrow?
Next week?
Before Christmas
Or next year?

Stephanie Grant (11)
Banff Primary School, Banff

Evacuee

Waiting at the train station is so sad
When you have to leave your mum and dad
It will feel weird in a different home
Especially when you are all alone

The family I am with is really kind
A little strict, you might find
They feed me really proper food
Which is really lovely and very good

The new house I am in is on a farm
So far there has been no harm
The view of the fields are lovely
Believe me, they are magnificent.

Leigh Killah (11)
Banff Primary School, Banff

World War II

Zoom, crash, splat, die
Spitfires are flying high
People not stopping by
Zoom, crash, splat, die
Britain getting ready to fly
Lost people are about to die
Zoom, crash, splat, die
Hitler we are going to win
We're going to make you stand on a pin
Zoom, crash, splat, die
Lots of blood and guts are flying high
Hitler *bang, bang,* you're going to die!

Kieren Macphee (11)
Banff Primary School, Banff

I Am An Evacuee

I am an evacuee
Standing by the trains
I am an evacuee
Someone's calling my name

I am scared and frightened
With my gas mask slung over my shoulder
I am scared and frightened
Standing there getting colder and colder

A woman took me away
She looked quite horrid and cruel
A woman took me away
She showed me my new school

Her house is big and clean
I've got a room all for my own
Her house is big and clean
I am not alone

All the kids are looking very sad
All the kids are looking
All thinking I'm evil and bad

The war is over
Hitler is dead
All I'm looking forward to
Is seeing my family and bed.

Meghan Coady (11)
Banff Primary School, Banff

WORLD WAR II

War is here,
Faces full of fear,
People are scared
Now that war has been declared.

Men go to fight
For the country's right,
If they die,
Their families will cry.

On the train, evacuees in tears,
It's the only way to forget about their fears,
The train has come to a stop
And people's ears *pop.*

At their new homes
Some evacuees sleep,
Others worry and start to count sheep,
In the morning, they use their combs.

The war has ended
And Hitler's dead,
The Russian army
Made him shoot his head.

Laura Barr (11)
Banff Primary School, Banff

WAR HAS ARRIVED

Oh no, World War II has arrived
I'm sad, I'm lonely, I'm terrified
I can't sing a song or play a game
Because it'll never be the same

I have to live in another home
I've got no one, I'm so alone
I'll miss my family and my friends
I hope World War II soon ends

We have to be as quiet as a mouse
Or Hitler will bomb the house
In my head I'm asking why
Are so many innocent people about to die?

Demi Mair (11)
Banff Primary School, Banff

SPACE TRAVEL

I see Saturn,
I see Mars,
Among the planets
And the stars.

All the planets round the sun,
Circling round seems like fun.
Too many stars sparkling brightly,
Always dark, always nightly.

Then I go back to the ground,
Landing softly without a sound.
When I get out of my rocket,
I find a moon rock in my pocket.

Tom Seed
Banff Primary School, Banff

Larry And Harry

Larry is small,
Larry is thin,
Harry is huge
And I love him.

Larry's face is pointed,
Harry's face is round.

Larry's hair is short,
Harry's hair is long.

Larry's tail is always wagging,
Harry's tail is always down.

Larry has brown ears,
So does Harry and sorry,
Larry and Harry are dogs.

Lauren Clarke (8)
Banff Primary School, Banff

Sam And Harry

Harry is small, thin and gentle,
Sam is large and fat,
But they're my two dogs.

Their faces are so smooth,
Harry's is long, thin and pointed,
Sam's is short and tired, so droopy.

Harry's hair is thin and short,
Sam's hair is straight and long.

Joseph Jeffrey (8)
Banff Primary School, Banff

Thin Jim And Fat Sam

Thin Jim is long,
Fat Sam is chubby,
I like them because they're lovely!

Jim's nose is pointed,
Sam's is round,
I like them because they were found . . .
In the pound!

Sam's tail is too little,
Jim's is too big,
Their hair is the same,
Tuggy and tangled,
But they're cool, cool, *cool!*

Steven MacDonald (8)
Banff Primary School, Banff

Tom And Bill

Tom is little
Bill is big

Tom's face is smooth
Bill's face is hairy

Tom's hair is brown
Bill's hair is white

Tom's tail is small and waggy
Bill's tail is short and shaggy.

Rebecca Anderson (9)
Banff Primary School, Banff

Hoopy And Jimmy

Hoopy is tiny
Hoopy is long
Hoopy is sometimes a little bit loopy

Jimmy is enormous
Jimmy is chubby
Jimmy is sometimes a little bit hummy

Hoopy's tail is straight, long and waggy
Jimmy's is short and not waggy,
But they are cool.

Hoopy's hair is short,
Jimmy's is long and tangled,
But I love them.

Hoopy's a pet,
Jimmy's a guard dog
And they keep me safe.

Stacey Murphy (8)
Banff Primary School, Banff

Spaceship

Spaceship, spaceship, over there
Watching, watching everywhere,
Like a bird, only soaring higher,
In our solar system.

Rachael A Hay (10)
Banff Primary School, Banff

Goldie And Samantha

Samantha is a horse
And Goldie is too,
I love them very much,
Don't you?

Samantha's face is very smooth
And it's happy,
With square teeth
That are very chatty.

Goldie's face is very rough
And it's very sad,
With square teeth
That are very nice and shiny too.

Samantha's hair is short and sleek
And makes her very sweet.
Goldie's hair is dirty and matted,
It makes her look a mess,
When Samantha's hair is very nice,
I'm impressed!

Siobhan McAllister (8)
Banff Primary School, Banff

Mars

M ars is a planet that may have life
A planet with volcanoes, not very hot; known as the
R ed planet, rusting away day by day the
S un is not too far away.

Connon Mackenzie (10)
Banff Primary School, Banff

Ben And Butch

Ben is long
Ben is little
Butch is enormous
And I like him

Ben's nose is pointed
Butch's is black
And they have wet noses

Ben's hair is soft
Ben's hair is shiny
Butch's hair is tangly
But I still love him

Ben's tail is waggy
Ben's tail is straight
Butch's tail is stubby and short
But they are still lovely

Ben's legs are short
Ben's feet are small
Butch's legs are long
Butch's feet are big
But I don't care.

Adele Buchan (8)
Banff Primary School, Banff

Space

Rockets zooming up so high
Up to space in the sky
Milky Way passing by
Too fast to catch my eye

I land on Mars
I hope to see
ET, the alien
Chasing me

Landing on Earth
With a bump
ET waving down to me
I am glad I got free.

Andrew Walker (10)
Banff Primary School, Banff

Jupiter

J upiter is the king of all the planets
U nlike Earth, Jupiter is mostly gas
P luto is tiny compared to Jupiter
I wonder if there is a planet bigger than Jupiter out there?
T he Romans named Jupiter after their king of gods
E arth is dwarfed compared to Jupiter
R omans were probably excellent astronomers.

Kristofer Alexander (10)
Banff Primary School, Banff

If I Were An Astronaut

If I were an astronaut
I'd be in space,
If I were an astronaut
I'd think it's ace!
In space there are aliens,
Black holes and stars,
Other spaceships and crew,
With planets like Mars.
I like space,
It's really vast,
I like space,
It will always last.
If I were an astronaut
I'd take up my friends,
If I were an astronaut
The fun would never end.
If I were an astronaut
I'd be in space,
If I were an astronaut
I'd think it's ace!

Jamie Davies (11)
Banff Primary School, Banff

Viking

Vikings rowing in long ships,
Viking stealing treasure,
Vikings killing monks,
Vikings are fierce with their swords and shields,
Fighting through England.

Kieran MacGregor (8)
Banff Primary School, Banff

My Spaceship

I wish I had a spaceship,
I'd fly up into space,
I'd go to every planet
And visit every place.

I'd fly my ship,
Close to the sun,
But before it fried me,
I'd be well and truly gone.

Then I'd start falling
And I'd feel quite sad,
Because my excellent journey
Is just another dream I've had.

Iain McKean (10)
Banff Primary School, Banff

Planets

P eaceful and colourful,
L onely and silent,
A mazing in lots of different ways,
N ight sky is glittering with shining stars,
E arth is so far away,
T he beautiful sky never ends,
S wirling stars all over the place.

Nicola Cook (10)
Banff Primary School, Banff

Space Travel

The spacecraft is shuddering,
It's getting ready to take-off,
The astronauts are nervous,
The engine is burning and steaming,
It's about to explode.

Booooom!
The spacecraft has lift-off,
The engine is burning,
It cuts through the air at the speed of light,
People below are clapping.

As the spacecraft enters orbit, it slows down,
The stars are bright and colourful,
The Earth looks *big* up, up above,
As the journey comes to an end.

The astronauts are glad to be going back to Earth,
The spacecraft changes direction and heads for Earth,
The astronauts look out the window,
They see the city small and people tiny,
As they land there's a giant *splasssh.*

Andrew Mathieson (10)
Banff Primary School, Banff

Astronaut

I am an astronaut flying in space
I float around the galaxy leaving no trace
When I see the big red sun
Suddenly the journey becomes more fun

My favourite thing is when you close your eyes
When you open them there's stars in the sky
No gravity is fun when you're in space
Only if nothing hits your face

When the space rocket circles the moon
You know you'll be arriving on Earth soon
When giant asteroids come your way
You want a hero to save the day.

Stuart Murray (10)
Banff Primary School, Banff

I'd Like To Go Into Space

I'd like to go into space,
To see all the other planets,
I'd go up in a spaceship
And move swiftly away from Earth.

I'd like to go into space,
To see Earth from far away,
I'd land on every planet
And land on every moon.

I'd like to go into space,
To see how big it really is,
I'd take home some moon rock,
For everyone to see.

Catherine Knowlson (10)
Banff Primary School, Banff

Adventure Up In Space!

Space is an adventure
There's a lot to do
Unlike the Earth
Plain, boring and blue

Space is cool
Space is fun
Floating everywhere near the sun

Space is colourful
Twinkling stars
Shining brightly
Near Mars.

Faye Smith (10)
Banff Primary School, Banff

Spaceship!

S ometimes I have a dream,
P eople talk about the solar system,
A n encouragement to ride a spaceship,
C ome on, let's go!
E njoy the ride,
S even, six, five, four, three, two, one, blast-off!
H ave an amazing time,
I hope that I do too!
P lease don't wake up! But then my amazing trip has ended!

Michael McGregor (10)
Banff Primary School, Banff

SPACE POEMS

Spaceships are terribly dull and grey,
What will they be like years from today?
Silver and sleek,
Or still antique.

It sits up straight,
It looks great,
Until blast-off,
The black dust rises like a Goth.

In the future, they'll be quiet,
There's no need for a riot,
'Wake up, wake up,' says Dad,
I've been daydreaming, now I'm mad.

Jon Watson (10)
Banff Primary School, Banff

PLANETS

P lanets are huge
L ots of moons
A nd all sizes
N ever forget there are nine
E verybody lives on Earth
T here is Mercury, Venus, Earth, Mars, Jupiter
S aturn, Uranus, Neptune and tiny Pluto.

Keith Rennie (10)
Banff Primary School, Banff

METEORS

I am an egg that never hatches,
I am a ball that never bursts,
I have water inside me, but it's frozen
So it won't quench your thirst.

I'm a bullet that travels at the speed of light,
Am I a silver bullet? No, not quite.

I whizz past a planet,
I whizz past the stars,
I zoom under Saturn's rings,
I whizz past quasars.

I am a meteor,
A whizzing space rock,
I travel as fast as I want,
I don't need your clock.

Andrew Davidson (10)
Banff Primary School, Banff

PLANETS

P luto is the smallest planet,
L ittle as a small bead,
A ll the planets are round,
N o one would think of it,
E arth is the planet we live on,
T he only planet to breathe,
S pace is the place to go to.

Jennifer Gordon (10)
Banff Primary School, Banff

Gerbils

Gerbils are fluffy, warm and cute
With soft fur and twitchy noses
Their paws are tickly on your hands
That makes you laugh for ages

Gerbils come in different colours
Such as brown and white
They come in different shapes and sizes
Such as small and big

Gerbils have small, shiny eyes
And very long tails
They sometimes even trip themselves up!

Gerbils are so cute and warm
You wish you could see every
Gerbil in the world.

Scott Shearer (8)
Banff Primary School, Banff

Pencils

Pencils are for drawing round stencils,
Red, green, yellow, all different kinds of colours,
Big pencils and small,
Thousands for all,
Pencils with rubbers at the top,
Make sure you don't drop them
When your mum is using the mop,
Colouring pencils and writing pencils,
Pencils are useful,
Pencils, pencils, pencils.

Kieran Alexander (9)
Banff Primary School, Banff

ROCK AND ROLL

Rock and roll, come on let's go!
I like to rock! I like to roll!
Come one, it's roll and rock,
Rock and roll, come on let's go.

We'll dance to the rock,
We'll sing to the roll,
Let's twist and turn,
Go high and low.

Come on, sing to the music,
Dance to the beat,
Move your hands and
Move your feet.

Rock and roll, come on let's go!
I like to rock! I like to roll!
Come on, it's roll and rock,
Rock and roll, come on let's go.

Kerr Baptie (8)
Banff Primary School, Banff

FRIENDS

Friends are nice to each other
They play together
I like to see people get on with each other
They help each other
They help you if you're stuck on a word.

Shannan Gallon (8)
Banff Primary School, Banff

WAR

Bang! Bang! Bang!
The bombs explode
Crashing down
Leaving homes destroyed

Bang! Bang! Bang!
Men go to war
Fight for our country
Scared, frightened and afraid

I don't want to go away
I want to stay
I want to feel safe
But I don't want to feel upset.

Stephanie Skinner (11)
Banff Primary School, Banff

WORLD WAR II

Hitler's mental, Hitler's mad
And he's done something really bad,
Britain's at war, fighting for freedom,
I hope they win because we need them.

Bombs are flying,
People are dying,
Children are crying,
Stop the war
Or deal with Hitler,
He's bad.

Samantha Morrison (11)
Banff Primary School, Banff

World War II

Zoom, crash, bang, fly
Lots of people are going to die
People crying all around

Zoom, crash, bang, fly
Lots of children are going to die
Blood and guts are flying high

Zoom, crash, bang, fly
Lots of planes are flying high
Dropping bombs and lighting the sky

Zoom, crash, bang, fly
Pilots are dying whilst they fly
Up high in the dark night sky.

Daniel Ewen (11)
Banff Primary School, Banff

Elephants

E normous,
L arge ears,
E ndangered,
P eaceful,
H abit of eating a lot,
A daptable,
N oble,
T usks made of ivory,
S trong.

Graeme Martin (8)
Banff Primary School, Banff

SPACE

I'd like to go up into space,
Visit all the stars.
See the rings of Saturn,
Take a bite out of Mars.

I'd see the volcanoes of Venus,
Go along the Milky Way,
See all of the planets that I know,
Even though there's more, they say.

To see the giant Jupiter,
That would be a dream.
I'd like to step on Uranus,
That would be supreme.

I can't go up to the sun,
Because all I'd do is burn.
I would have to jump to Mercury
And there I would then burn.

Patrick Fisher (10)
Banff Primary School, Banff

MONDAY

M onday is a boring day,
O n Monday I had maths,
N o, I am not going to school tomorrow,
D on't make me go to school today
A nd my mum made me go to school,
Y esterday I had a great day.

John Sloan (8)
Banff Primary School, Banff

My Fantasy Dream

I'd like to go into space,
To try to avoid the human race,
I will read a book,
To help be a cook.

Making bacon for the stars,
Then they'll be taking me over to Mars.
They'll be fast as the speed of light,
They'll be so fast I might get a fright.

It'll be really cold, I might get old,
Or even find some gold,
But these are my dreams
And I'm still in Earth, so it seems.

Ashleigh Strain (10)
Banff Primary School, Banff

Dogs Barking

A long bow-wow
Find our puppies, find them now
They have got short fluffy ears
Dark black spots
And eyes as clear as a stone

A short bow-wow
We have found your puppies
Come right now
They have got short fluffy ears
Dark black spots
And eyes as clear as a stone.

Nicole Knott (8)
Banff Primary School, Banff

MEMORIES

I'm waiting at the station, I'm sad
I've got to go and leave my mum and dad
I go on the train, I shed a tear
I'm so scared and full of fear

I arrive at last
I walk off the train fast
I stand by myself all alone
I hope I get picked and go to a good home

This lady comes over
I hold my lucky clover
Now I can see
She's looking at me

She takes me away
'Thank you' I say
That was many years ago
There's one thing I know
I will always remember
The year 1939, the sad month of September.

Emma-Louise Reid (11)
Banff Primary School, Banff

VIKINGS, VIKINGS

There's a Viking over there,
With a fiery red beard and a very sharp sword,
With a very funny-looking shield,
There's a Viking over there.

Eight little Viking children learning to fight,
They are very competitive.

Milo Mole (8)
Banff Primary School, Banff

Space

The astronaut looked out the window,
He was surprised to see a bright green man,
Shining like a shooting star,
The man was on a glittering asteroid,
Then he noticed something came and changed,
The lights went out and the floor went *creak*,
The door opened and the astronaut fainted.

The astronaut woke up in a building in another galaxy,
His digital watch was wrong,
It said he had been asleep for 2000 years,
The astronaut didn't look a day older than 25,
He felt a shiver down his spine,
Something was coming, the door opened,
An alien opened the door and it used a needle on the astronaut,
He was never seen again.

Mark Cole (10)
Banff Primary School, Banff

Monday

M onday is a very boring day,
O n Monday I have maths to do.
N o, I'm not going to school on Monday,
D on't make me do that on Monday,
A re you going to school on Monday?
Y esterday I went swimming.

Sarah Barr (8)
Banff Primary School, Banff

SPACE

Rockets speeding through the air,
Dodging asteroids up and down.
Stopping at every strange planet,
What are they doing? Nobody knows.

Twinkling stars, shining brightly,
On their way back they find spaceships.
Loads of aliens in them,
Astronauts float away to who knows where.

Now they are landing on a planet,
They have landed on Pluto.
'There is no sign of life,' they said
And started their journey back to Earth.

Ryan Buchan (10)
Banff Primary School, Banff

WAR!

Men going off to war
For years and years
Up, two, three, four!
Captains shouting!
Blood there and everywhere!
Guns going *bang! Bang!*
People shouting, 'Die, die for us.'
Tanks killing people like mad!
Bodies everywhere.

Scott Mathieson (8)
Banff Primary School, Banff

FLOWERS

Flowers, there are flowers over there
Flowers everywhere

Flowers smell wonderful
Daffodils smell of lemons
And you can smell them from anywhere
Even when you're in your car
You smell them anywhere

Flowers are any colour,
Blue, pink, purple, yellow or red
They come out of the rainbow.

Amy Gatt (8)
Banff Primary School, Banff

ROUGHY TOUGHY

Roughy Toughy
Just so rough
He's so fat
He's my pet dog
Roughy Toughy
He's my brown bulldog
He's got the biggest cheeks
And so floppy
And little eyes.

Cameron McAllister (8)
Banff Primary School, Banff

SPACE

An astronaut floating on the moon
Bouncing in plenty of room
Spaceships flying, stars twinkling
Aliens landing and speeding rockets
What a wonderful place to be
Different planets, red and green

Ground control sends a message
Come back to Earth
The journey is long and people worry
But we get safely home
Out we step on planet Earth
Back to all our family and friends.

Kieran Morrison (10)
Banff Primary School, Banff

SPACE

Stars and the sun are twinkling in the galaxy,
Asteroid floating,
Aliens are hiding in the Milky Way,
I know something's wrong with the ozone layer.

Mercury and Pluto are the smallest planets in space,
As I stare at the sky, something is gleaming.
I notice it is a flying star,
I see there is peace in the sky,
As long as I live my life, I know I'll be happy.

James Mackintosh (10)
Banff Primary School, Banff

HITLER, THE MAD, THE VERY BAD

Hitler was a weird
Stupid man
He did things
That were awful, bad
His parents did not raise him well
So Hitler was brought up
To be really
Mad
When Hitler started the war
It made me very sad
Hitler caused a stupid war
That's why I think he is
Bad
I am a soldier
I hate Hitler
He killed my children
And my wife
Jane
That's why I think Hitler's a pain
If you ask me
I'd say he is insane
I hate you Hitler
You stupid, silly, crazy man.

Martin Mitchell (12)
Banff Primary School, Banff

My Dog, Bracken

I remember the day I was in the car going to get him,
I was very excited and had a big grin,
Every morning I was very sad,
'Cause I had to leave him,
I thought that was very bad,
In the car on my way to school,
I would be crying, like I was in a swimming pool!
Then came the day I had to sell him,
He was crying, so was I,
While tickling under his chin,
A week later, I visited him at his new house,
He was jumping with joy, not like a mouse,
I really miss Bracken and I wish he were here right now.

Ashley Hall (11)
Banff Primary School, Banff

The Vikings

Vikings in a long-boat sailing on the sea
Hoist the sail and off we go
The Vikings invade Lindisfarne
And lots of people were killed

The monks were terrified
The Vikings stole some gold and silver from the church
The Vikings went back to Scandinavia
And left a bunch of dead bodies
Lying around the floors.

Jordon Reid (8)
Banff Primary School, Banff

My Pets

My dog might chase my cat
My cat might chase my mouse
My mouse just eats the crumbs
That he finds around the house

My dog sleeps in a kennel
My cat sleeps on my bed
My mouse just sleeps anywhere
As long as he's been fed

My dog just wants to play
My cat just wants to sleep
My mouse just wants to eat all day
And that's how things are going to stay.

Laurence Woods (11)
Banff Primary School, Banff

Space

Astronauts go up and look at the planet
Glittery, shiny, shooting stars,
Zooming past my brand new car.

Food tubes that look like toothpaste,
But taste scrummy yummy,
With aliens that have jagged teeth
And some with stripes and spots or patches.

Quietly they creep and hide in craters,
Slowly and steady they creep along,
They stare at us far away,
With eyes on stalks that move about.

Amy Yorkston (10)
Banff Primary School, Banff

Up In Space

We're on our journey up to space
'Can you guess which is the alien's face?
Can you?'

'I can't,' he said.
'I wish I could lie and slop in bed.'

I wish I could, but I can't just yet,
I wish I could bring my little cat pet.

Up to space we get, in an hour,
The planets look like they've spun in flour.

The moon looks like a rotten sponge,
The rest look like they've rolled in gunge.

So that's our journey over with now,
I like the planets but I don't know how.

Vicky Noble (11)
Banff Primary School, Banff

Up In Space

Aliens have their dinner,
Martians have a game of football
And the flying saucers have a race.
The aliens have finished their dinner,
The Martians have finished their game of football,
They all meet up to watch the TV.

Daniel Thomson (10)
Banff Primary School, Banff

THE SPACEMAN

There was an astronaut who went into space
And started walking at the wrong pace
He floated off to the stars
And fell on the side of Mars

Then he went back to Venus
And went back to his rocket
Then pulled out of his pocket
His radio to contact Earth
The only place he contacted was Perth

He started up the rocket
And flew down to Earth
But landed not in Perth
He landed in Banff
And he went out of his rocket
Then pulled out of the other pocket a map
And then said, 'I need a nap,'
So he went back in the rocket

When he woke up
Then soon got up
And went outside
He saw a great big slide
Then all of a sudden he woke up again
And knew it was all a dream
Then he had strawberries and cream.

Sophie Pellett (10)
Banff Primary School, Banff

Space

Stars are twinkling as bright as the sun
And the galaxies are spiralling in motion
Astronauts are floating in the moon's law gravity
And the satellite is flying round the Earth's atmosphere

Mercury is orbiting the sun faster than the Earth
And the sun is burning hotter than a cooker on full blast
Aliens are maybe on Mars or any other planets
Space has mysteries still to be discovered
I wonder what they are?

Gavin Watt (10)
Banff Primary School, Banff

Journey To Space

Twinkling stars float all over space
They shoot and dart all over the place
There are planets, there are nine
They twist and twirl and sometimes shine
Nobody knows the mystery of space
How it got there in the very first place

Astronauts go to space in their rockets
Hoping to come back with things in their pockets
Could there be aliens up there in the gloom?
Waiting and watching from my little blue room

5, 4, 3, 2, 1, *blast-off!*

Jonathon Gatt (10)
Banff Primary School, Banff

Space Invasion

An alien floats down from the sky
But I say to myself
Is it an illusion or real?
I hide in the deep moon crater

There were big spaceships
As black as night
But the stars were as bright
As a big yellow light

One of the aliens saw me
And said, 'Who are you?'
I didn't give him my real name
I said I was, 'Bond, James Bond'

He said to his strange, spooky, green friends
'Intruder' they all ran away
They all got into their spaceships
It was a really scary day.

Jason Smith (10)
Banff Primary School, Banff

Rangers

R angers are the best, yes they
A re, dare them to a challenge you'll
N ever beat them for all they do is score
G oals, goals, goals
E verywhere they go, you'll see a goal
R icksen is the best winger you'll see
S o never challenge them to a match.

Christopher Davidson (11)
Banff Primary School, Banff

Off To The Moon

Off to the moon, I go so soon,
5, 4, 3, 2, 1, blast-off!
I fly into space at an astounding pace.
I whizz so fast, I don't see all the countries go past,
I can see the sun, it looks like a hot cross bun,
When I look to the right, I see the sun so bright.

My lunar ship lands on the moon,
I start to walk like a Looney Toon.
I float along the rock like a small piece of chalk,
I whizz off the moon and get home alone,
I get back and start to walk like an alien drone.

Ross Bligdon (10)
Banff Primary School, Banff

Aliens And Rockets

Flying rockets zooming upside down,
Flying round and round, making funny noises,
All the children watching
And running round and round.

Shooting stars shine in the night sky,
Comets zooming through the twinkly sky.
Glittery ones purple and blue,
Make the sky beautiful.

Aliens with moon buggies zooming through space,
Watching TV with your satellite dish.
Aliens with mates eat chicken and gravy,
Dribbling gravy down their green chin.

Kelly-Anne Innes (10)
Banff Primary School, Banff

A Journey To Space

Getting in a rocket, feeling fine,
Looking at the clock, watching the time.
5, 4, 3, 2, 1, *blast-off!* We're off to space,
You should see the look of the driver's face.
His cheeks go red, his eyes start to shimmer,
He shouts, 'We're going to see the stars glimmer.'
A day has passed, doesn't time fly,
I see a comet shooting by.

I look at the planets some have rings
And a few have other things.
I see the sun, it looks very burny,
Oh no, it's almost the end of my journey.
We land on the moon, it looks like cheese,
The driver looks very pleased.
He plants a flag on the moon,
He says, 'This is for mankind who will live here soon.'

Peter Day (10)
Banff Primary School, Banff

Space

I stare up to space and block out the world,
Not a care in my mind, not a care in the world.

I dream of flying through the galaxy,
Exploring space and gravity.

Exploring the galaxy that is my place,
I want to fly through deepest space.

Paul Stuart (10)
Banff Primary School, Banff

Space Poem

People live on Earth
In a place called Perth
Astronauts go in space
Flying there at such a pace

Children in bed
When Mars is red
Pluto is blue
And friends like you

Snow is white
And stars are bright
Mercury is brown
And the king wears a crown.

Rosemary Coles (10)
Banff Primary School, Banff

The Beach

The beach is fun,
You can build sandcastles,
You can look in rock pools,
For crab and starfish.
As the tide comes in,
The rock pool disappears,
The sandcastles start to crumble
And the waves cover the beach.
When the tide comes in I feel sad
It covers the rock pool and the sandcastles.
My castle building is ruined and
My rock pool friends have moved.

Darryl Duncan (11)
Banff Primary School, Banff

MY BEST FRIENDS' CATS!

My best friend, Ashley
Has a cat called Mitzy,
Who gets a little bit itchy.

My best friend, Dionne
Has a cat called Jasper,
Who is scared of Casper.

My best friend, Lucy
Has a cat called Smarty,
It likes to party.

My best friend, Lucy
Has a cat called Tiger,
Who drank cider at Smarty's party!

Jenna Killoh (11)
Banff Primary School, Banff

TOYOTA CELICA

T oyota Celica
O il
Y esterday we went for a spin
O utside, beside the castle
T owards the traffic lights
A t green

C ruising around
E xhaust
L eaves the bottom of the car
I nside the stereo blasts
C rash
A gainst the wall.

Martyn Shand (11)
Banff Primary School, Banff

My Best Friend!

Eilidh is my best friend,
Our friendship will never end.
Her name is Eilidh Fiona Walker,
She is a very fast talker.
She has short brown hair
And we make a great pair.

She has ten pets,
They hate the vets.
Her eyes are blue,
Mine are too.
We've having a sleepover on Friday,
Games of truth and dare we'll play.

We go shopping and to the pool,
Eilidh is very cool,
She is clever.
Sarah and Eilidh, best friends forever.
At her house we walk the dogs, watch TV,
Talk and talk, just her and me.

We dance around the living room,
But then I go home too soon,
I say goodbye and go away,
I come back again another day
And she's my best friend.

Sarah Murray (11)
Banff Primary School, Banff

BAMBI!

Bambi is my pony,
She is a very lovely sight,
With a chestnut coat and four white socks,
She is the cutest thing in time.

When we go on holiday,
All I think of is her,
She is a star in my heart,
When I lay in my bed at night,
I wonder what she does.

Maybe she stays up until 12am
And then snuggles into a thick bed of straw.
Bambi is the best horse ever,
Even though she is 30,
I will always love her better than the rest.

Lucy Montrose (11)
Banff Primary School, Banff

HORSES

Horses gallop through waves
Clip-clop, clip-clop
Trotting in the water fast as they can
Clip-clop, clip-clop
Horses gallop back to the stable
Clip-clop, clip-clop.

Michaela Ure (8)
Banff Primary School, Banff

SPIDERS

S piders are pretty cool,
P eople don't like spiders,
I do,
D on't kill a spider or it will rain the next day,
E veryone is scared of spiders
R eally they're not that bad,
S o next time you see a spider just remember it won't go near you.

S piders are pretty much harmless,
P eople think that spiders will bite,
I think that spiders are nice,
D own the back of my shed you will find a big web,
E ven bigger than a plate,
R ight up the wall a spider can go,
S o next time you see a spider just remember spiders don't bite.

Jamie Wilson (11)
Banff Primary School, Banff

FRIENDS

Friends help me with my maths
Friends play with me
Friends help me with my English
Friends share things
Friends help me with my homework.

Allan Cook (8)
Banff Primary School, Banff

People Loving

Love is beautiful,
Love is nice,
Love is like a red, red rose,
Bright and beautiful like my love
And she smells like a beautiful flower,
Her face is like a delicate flower
And her hair is so smooth.

Emma Pantel (8)
Banff Primary School, Banff

The Monster

I like monsters with spots a lot
They also have big blots
A monster with spots and big blots
Went to the shop and bought some hot sauce
It was so hot, he got four more dots.

Neil Anderson (9)
Clatt Primary School, Huntly

The Christmas Tree

Oh Christmas tree
Oh Christmas tree
Oh how the wind does blow
With the snow
Oh your light looks so bright
Under the moonlight.

Michelle Connon (7)
Clatt Primary School, Huntly

The Moon

The moon is round
and as white as cheese.
I like watching stars
while I freeze.

Francesca Walsh (9)
Clatt Primary School, Huntly

Space

Space is ace
You can fly to the moon
In a rocket with a *boom*
Having a space race
I never stop for a rest
In the middle of a race.

Andrew Chalmers (10)
Clatt Primary School, Huntly

A Football Poem

When I'm in goal
I catch and throw
Feel and hold
Big and bold.

John Connon (10)
Clatt Primary School, Huntly

THE BULLY

Silence
The whole playground watches
Echoing footsteps
The bully approaches
His eyes shining
His fists clenched
Now I know I'm the victim

His shadow blocks the sun
The heat drains from me
A piercing scream
A stabbing pain
A tear runs down my cheek
The bully's back at school.

Jessica Wright (10)
Crombie Primary School, Westhill

THE BULLY

A hideous grin
His arms so huge and tough
He is like a dog fighting a cat
'I'll get you,' he yelled
Like a leopard he runs
And punches my face

An unhappy face
Legs like jelly, I can't run
I wish I were a monkey to swing out of reach
I howl, 'Please don't!'
But it was too late
Crunch! into my face.

Lisa McCarrol (10)
Crombie Primary School, Westhill

The Horror

Gnashing teeth,
Coal black eyes,
Breathing like a rusty saw,
Trapping its prey,
Narrowing his eyes,
He stomps loudly,
Ready to pounce,
Clenched fists ready to punch,
Going in for the kill,
'Ready or not, here I come,' he spits,
Pouncing like a bobcat,
He soars like an eagle,
Shooting faster than a bullet,
He catches his prey,
Lifting his mighty hand,
He strikes,
He is happy with his work.

Crying for mercy, I beg,
But getting none whatsoever,
I take slow steps backwards,
Eyes as big as full moons,
Face as clear as crystal,
Arms as thin as thread,
Voice as croaky as a frog's,
Wishing I was ill,
I tried to ignore him,
But my eyes were fixed on him,
'No, please I will do anything,' I croak,
Too late, I'm hit,
I am sick with pain.

Stuart McMaster (10)
Crombie Primary School, Westhill

The Bully Vs Me

Big, bulging eyes like planets up in space,
His fists are ready to shoot his goal,
He says, 'Are you scared? Because you'd better be!'
This bully is like an eagle finding some prey,
Away he goes,
His fist shooting like a rocket up in space,
He shoots, he scores.

My knees unstable, quivery, precarious,
My teeth are chattering,
I feel like I could cry,
Maybe I will, I really can't,
I feel like a fool,
His fist is coming,
I can't move!
He hits, the pain!

Danielle Allan (10)
Crombie Primary School, Westhill

Love

Love is red, the colour of the rose,
Love tastes like the sweet red wine,
Love smells like the lovely jam tarts,
Love looks like the birds flying high outside,
Love sounds like the children laughing in the sun,
Love feels like the silky red heart.

Leanne Wilson (10)
Crombie Primary School, Westhill

The Bully And Me

The bully kicks and punches,
With nasty concentration.
Ruthless energy,
Hard-hearted grin.
He chases me like cat and mouse,
Hunted down.
'Jennifer, you're dead!'
I wait,
For my fate.

Always scared is the victim,
I don't make a noise,
Stand really still.
My face stone-cold,
There is no place to worry or cry,
I think that I am going to die!

Jennifer Park (10)
Crombie Primary School, Westhill

Happiness

Happiness is yellow, as bright as the sun,
It tastes like strawberries and cream,
It smells like a sweet red rose,
Happiness sounds like the laughter of children,
It feels warm like the taste of hot chocolate,
It looks like a vast field of daffodils.

Lynsey Irvine (10)
Crombie Primary School, Westhill

The Bully

He grins
His eyebrows pushed together
Smiling with a menacing look
'I'll be done with you someday!' he sneers
He pushes with clenched fists
Ready to run at me!
Like a cheetah he pounces
Wallop!
He laughs

'Help!' - I squeaked
My teeth clenching
My eyes numb
I started to walk with fear
Holding my hips
My body felt tight
As he punched me
I was bulging with fear
I stuttered *'Stop!'*

Faye Cumming (10)
Crombie Primary School, Westhill

THE BULLY

A devil's grin,
His fists like rocks,
His tall dark figure lingers over me.
His name, Brock the Rock,
Known by all the school as 'the bully'.
'I'm coming to get you!' he shouts menacingly.
Crunch!
The time has come,
Fist to stomach.

My mouth an upside-down smile,
Arms are like jelly,
My small, dark figure stick-like,
I'm called Frances or 'the wimp',
Known by most people as 'the wimp'.
'Don't hurt me!' I yell,
But I'm too late.
I get the full blow from his powerful fist,
I'm so tired of this pain.

Kathryn Hunter (10)
Crombie Primary School, Westhill

THE BULLY!

A vicious frown
Dark brown vile eyes
His enormous arm appears on my shoulder
His fingernails clench into my arm like claws
Then suddenly he growls like a lion
Watch out!

It's too late
I'm lying on the ground
Help! I can't run and hide
Instead I lie on the ground like a mouse
He stands on my leg
The lunch bell rings
He runs away then stops and says
'I'll be back!'

Sophie Svensen (10)
Crombie Primary School, Westhill

LOVE

Love is red like a rose,
Love tastes like a red strawberry tart
With a red cherry on the top,
Love smells like the red sweet wine,
Love looks like a red heart beating,
Love sounds like morning birds cheeping,
Love feels cosy and warm like hot chocolate.

Robyn Hay (10)
Crombie Primary School, Westhill

THE BULLY

Eyes as evil as fire
A menacing smirk
A body like a gorilla
His fists clenched
Charging like a bull
'I'll get you!' he bellows
As he pounces like a tiger
Bang!
He catches his prey!

Eyes bloodshot with fear
A body like a plant rooted in the soil
Hands shaking wildly
Pinned to the wall like a poster
'I'm not worth it,' I screech
Thud!
It's too late!

Kerri Hendry (10)
Crombie Primary School, Westhill

ANGER

Anger is a dark fiery red dragon,
It tastes like bubbling soup,
Anger smells like burning toast
And looks like a volcano erupting,
Anger sounds like crashing plates,
It feels like heartburn.

Jordan Connell (10)
Crombie Primary School, Westhill

THE BULLY VS ME!

His eyes narrow,
I was in for it,
I had to hide,
His arms like gorillas,
The anger in his face,
His dirty legs like rhinos,
The sullen expression on his face,
He is looking,
Looking for me!
Then a *smack* and a *crack!*
His bowling ball fist hits my nose!

My eyes screw up,
I start to cry!
My knees feel like jelly,
I cannot walk,
My stick-like arms are trembling!
I am sick with pain,
Then I burst,
The agony, not again!
My nose starts bleeding and does not stop!

Clara-Jane Irvine (10)
Crombie Primary School, Westhill

The Bully

The grinding teeth,
The clenching fists
And huge arms,
Me and him, no one else,
The bell goes, he does not move one inch,
The intimidating grin falls far short of pleasant,
There is nothing to do,
Not one thing.
Bang!
Bleeding all over,
No one to help me.
He kicks and leaves.

My jelly-like knees,
Shaking all over,
The blood dripping onto my school clothes.
I couldn't move,
My legs like roots on a tree.
'Help, help!' I sobbed.
My voice echoed,
No one was there.

Iain Smith (10)
Crombie Primary School, Westhill

The Bully

His vicious grin,
Eyes like a hawk,
As fierce as can be,
His fist clenched,
Ready,
Crunch,
His fist is compressed against my face.

I have to escape,
I feel like a mouse,
I hurt, I ache,
Where can I run?
Where can I hide?
There's no safe place
To hide from the bully.

Hannah Svensen (10)
Crombie Primary School, Westhill

Greed

Greed is orange like a juicy tangerine,
It tastes like a huge banquet of delicious food
On the dining room table,
The smell of melting chocolate dripping from the pan,
It looks like a stack of presents waiting for you,
It sounds like the clinking of money being counted,
Greed feels like you need everything in the world!

Leila Smithers (10)
Crombie Primary School, Westhill

The Bully's Revenge

A vicious frown
Fists like boulders
Arms like tree trunks
A tiger ready to pounce
'I'll get you for that,' he screams
He pounces for his prey
Slam, his leg, my knee

Eyes bloodshot with fear
Teeth chattering
Hands sweaty
A mouse ready to run
'No you won't,' I yelp
Scurry, dodge, leap
Slam, his leg, my knee.

Matthew Hinton (10)
Crombie Primary School, Westhill

Happiness

Yellow is the colour of the bright summer sun,
The taste of the ice cream that we eat in summer,
The smell of the Christmas turkey,
It looks like the colours of summer,
It is the sound of children playing,
Happiness makes you feel good all over.

Ruth McGlashan (9)
Crombie Primary School, Westhill

THE BULLY VS ME

Clenched eyebrows,
A menacing stare,
Fists locked, ready to hurt,
Coming over to me, stamping down his feet,
Getting closer and closer and closer, then,
Bang, wallop, crunch!
On the ground, nose bleeding,
Walking away with a snigger.

Sweating eyebrows,
Eyes as big as slices of bread,
Hands in my pockets expecting the unexpected,
Then everything in my world came to an abrupt halt,
I was down on the ground,
My nose was bleeding,
The bell rang,
He stamped away,
'I'll be back,' he bellowed,
The bell saved me!

Daniel Ferguson (10)
Crombie Primary School, Westhill

The Bully

A fierce jaw, eyes like a wild boar,
Eyebrows like elastic bands,
Crouching fists ready to go,
Bang!
Arms as big as tree stubs,
Nose like a monkey's tongue.
'Hey you, you're going down!'
He trembles like an elephant trumpeting,
He runs like a cheetah gliding across for its prey,
Standing tall as a giraffe,
Bang! in my face.

A terrified face, big eyes like a seal,
A mouth as small as a fish,
'Please, please,' I beg in fear,
Terrified as a mouse,
Tiny timid legs shaking,
'Not again,'
Bang!
Same as usual.

Julia Bryce (10)
Crombie Primary School, Westhill

The Bully

A dirty grin,
Eyes like a warrior,
His fists clenched so tight
And standing oh so rigid.
'You can run but you can't hide,' he howls.
Like a leopard he sprints,
His claws are in my face!

Yes panic stricken,
Hands dripping with sweat,
Arms and legs trembling like jelly.
Like a mouse, I am chased,
'No, no, please don't,' I squeak,
But it is too late.
The pain, the agony,
'Please, just leave me alone!'

Mairi Farquharson (10)
Crombie Primary School, Westhill

Love

Love is like a bright pink room,
Love tastes like sweet strawberries in the summertime,
Love smells like lovely red roses,
It sounds like the laughter of the children in the playground,
Love feels warm and bubbly like a hot summer's day,
It looks like a large bunch of red roses.

Laura Watson (10)
Crombie Primary School, Westhill

Big Bully Vs Little Me

A vicious grin, large white bread teeth,
An irritating chuckle and lethal fists,
Bulging muscles through those alarming arms.
Fingernails like claws with dirt hiding under,
With those scruffy eyebrows and dinner plate eyes,
Bearing down on me.
'I will get you!' he bellows.
He runs like a lion hunting his prey, he pounced.
'Gotcha!'
He pushed with stone-like arms,
I fell, *bang!*

Small, beady eyes filled with fear,
A timid mouse with sweaty, shaky hands.
Tiny stick-like arms and bony wrists and knobbly knees,
Chattering teeth and a trembling lip.
'Help!' I squeak,
I leapt and cantered like a horse,
Ouch! With a bruise forming at my eye.

Karin Moir (10)
Crombie Primary School, Westhill

Sadness

Sadness is blue like running teardrops
It tastes like soggy toast
Sadness smells like salted water
It looks like everything is drifting away
Sadness sounds like someone crying in the distance
Sadness feels like you're falling down a bottomless pit.

Chris Robertson (10)
Crombie Primary School, Westhill

THE BULLY!

His dark eyes looked my way,
He stared and stared with his menacing look
His huge fist grew very strong,
He hit it off the other hand and said,
'Run . . . run . . . as fast as you can!'
He ran towards me like a wild galloping horse
And jumped on my back like a lion catching its prey!
As fast as a bullet he punched my face!

My lip trembled like jelly,
As he stared into my eyes.
I could do nothing but stand and stare,
Like a frozen computer,
As he scrambled towards me!
My knees started to shake as he jumped on my back
And gave me a mighty
Punch!

Roanna Scott (10)
Crombie Primary School, Westhill

ANGER

Anger is red like blood dripping from your finger
It tastes like boiling chips on your tongue
Anger smells like smoke from your burning toast
It looks like fire rushing through the forest
Anger sounds like a deafening scream from the baby who lost its bottle
It feels horribly burny and prickly.

Abbey Sproul (10)
Crombie Primary School, Westhill

BULLY BOY

An intimidating grin
Cracking fists
Unyielding muscles
Like a herd of elephants coming towards you!
'Run as fast as you can!' he roared.
Like a lion chasing its prey
Thud his hand, my nose!

Hear thudding
Numb fingers
Knobbly knees
Scars reopening with fear!
'Please, I'm only weak,'
That timid voice pleaded
Whack!
The pain, the agony rushing through my blood.

Emma Brewer (10)
Crombie Primary School, Westhill

HAPPINESS

Happiness is red like the red roses
Happiness tastes like a yummy strawberry tart
Happiness smells like fresh cut spring grass
Happiness looks like the glistening snow
Happiness sounds like the rounding of the children
Happiness feels like I'm just going to fly
In the light blue sky.

Kyle Cowin (10)
Crombie Primary School, Westhill

THE BULLY

His glaring eyes
Searching the playground
For something, then he ceased
Started sprinting like a cheetah
And he bellows, 'You're dead, shrimp!'
He catches up and his fist's in my face

My big, watery brown eyes
With my hands quivering
On my stick-like arms
'Spare me, please spare me!' I screeched
My legs were like jelly
But I still legged it
Then I was getting a lot slower
He was gaining on me
And eventually he got me
It was over.

Shaun Johnson (10)
Crombie Primary School, Westhill

EXCITEMENT

Yellow is like the bright sunshine on a nice warm day,
It tastes like the ice-cold ice cream going down your throat
It smells like the new house you have not seen,
It sounds like the busy town street at the market on a Saturday,
It feels like the bubble floating around your stomach.

Abbie Forsyth (10)
Crombie Primary School, Westhill

THE BULLY

A cruel stare,
A twisted smile,
His hands are in fists,
His feet are gently kicking the road.
'I'll get you,' he bellows,
'I'll break you,' he whispers.
I know I'm in trouble,
Like a tiger he pounces,
Then *crush!*

My eyes are wide,
My breath is fast,
The palms of my hands are sweaty,
My legs are like jelly.
I'm like a mouse, trembling all over.
A tear runs down,
My leg is in pain,
Please help!

Bethany Lawson (9)
Crombie Primary School, Westhill

FEAR

Fear is black like the darkness of the night,
Fear tastes like black burnt toast,
Fear smells like hot steaming petrol,
Fear looks like a ghost glowing in the dark,
Fear sounds like creaking footsteps heading towards me,
Fear feels like you've just been struck dumb.

Daniel Rodgers (10)
Crombie Primary School, Westhill

Bully Boy

Strong arms,
Steel grey eyes,
He's after me again -
What a surprise!
As full of himself as an
Overflowing glass of beer,
Like a bull he bellows,
'I'll huff and I'll puff
And I'll punch you right down!'
Me, racing, rushing, but no match,
I feel sick, scared and stricken,
He attacks,
Crunch, his foot as strong
As a sledge hammer, trips me up,
My hands get sweaty,
My eyes get round,
I hit the ground,
Punch, kick, bite.

Gemma Reid (10)
Crombie Primary School, Westhill

Happiness

Happiness is yellow, it's like the sun
It tastes like dripping hot toffee
It smells like freshly cut grass
It looks like a colourful rainbow
It sounds like children laughing
It feels like jumping puppies
I love being happy.

Rachael Nicol (10)
Crombie Primary School, Westhill

THE BULLY VS ME

A kick, a punch
A terrifying grin
Bulging muscles, huge fists
Legs so big, kicking mud
Eyebrows frowning
He's really mad and very bad
'Come here, you!' he bellows
As he pounces like a lion
Crunch! he thumps his eye

Chattering teeth, wobbly knees
Watery eyes about to cry
His heart beats quickly
He's too scared to move
He panics, he shivers and is petrified
Bang! he falls over
It is all over, but he will strike again.

Robert Elrick (10)
Crombie Primary School, Westhill

ANGER

Anger is orange like the volcano steaming to blow up,
It looks like the fire burning in your face,
It sounds like the children screaming in the playground,
It feels like the burning sensation thumping in your heart,
It tastes like biting your tongue,
It smells like the mustard drifting in the air.

Amy McTavish (10)
Crombie Primary School, Westhill

The Bully Vs Me

A menacing grin and terrifying eyes,
His fists like rocks and his kick makes his victims cry,
He barks at his victims, 'You are mine!'
He would chase you like a wild animal,
He would hunt you like a beast,
He catches you and *thump*, he hits you right in the face.

Wobbly knees, chattering teeth,
A nauseous look on the victim's face,
Tears drip from his eyes,
A fearful look as the bully approaches slowly,
With a big breath, you turn and run,
As you turn, a cold hand you feel on your shoulder,
It all goes dark,
You fall to your fate, you sweat and then *smack!*
It's *all over*.

Lewis Murchie (10)
Crombie Primary School, Westhill

Fear

Fear is black like the coal in the fire,
It tastes like expired milk,
It smells like an empty house needing cleaning,
It looks like the boy wimpering in the corner,
It sounds like the blood dripping from the body,
It feels like your legs are hollow.

Fraser Irvine (10)
Crombie Primary School, Westhill

The Bully

He stands there waiting,
His legs are rigid,
His eyes are sharp and miss no movement,
He does not move,
He is like a lion waiting for his prey,
Me!

I know he's waiting,
My legs are like jelly,
I turn my eyes to where he stands,
I move to where I am going, ignoring him,
I am like the zebra, is it working?
Has he stopped?
Yes!

Josephine Alexander (10)
Crombie Primary School, Westhill

Excitement

Excitement is the colour of bright yellow like the sun
Shining on a summer's day
Excitement smells like the sweet candyfloss underneath my chin
Excitement tastes like vanilla ice cream
Melting so sweetly in my mouth
Excitement looks like a rainbow with gold sparkles
Excitement sounds like all the happy birds laughing as they play
Excitement feels like my new sofa sitting in my bedroom
But best of all, excitement's in me.

Michael Watson (10)
Crombie Primary School, Westhill

The Bully

Big brown glaring eyes,
Watching my every move,
A menacing grin,
Pulling his sleeves up
And clutching his fists,
Running towards me like a lion prowling,
Shouting, 'Watch out, the bully's about!'
Smash! His huge fist crunched my face,
Then gives a villainous laugh!

Wide blue eyes,
Just staring at him,
My teeth chattering,
Legs and arms shaking like an earthquake,
The palm of my hand sweating,
I run as fast as I can.
'Oh no! Don't hit me!' I squeak.
Crunch! A huge fist hits my face
And I cry in tears.

Rebecca Paterson (11)
Crombie Primary School, Westhill

Anger

Anger is red like blood
Anger tastes like horrible medicine
Anger smells like burning
Anger looks like lava falling from the volcano
Anger sounds like screams
Anger feels like my blood bubbling inside me.

Reece Manson (10)
Crombie Primary School, Westhill

THE BULLY

Eyes like dark tunnels,
Powerful as a wild boar,
His barrel chest sticking out,
Suddenly, arms raised, he turns,
Breathing rigidly,
He strikes with the power of a rhino,
A mischievous grin and freakish haircut,
Makes you want to scream, cry, anything,
Just to get away from him.

Eyes like marbles,
His frail stick-like body shivering uncontrollably,
As the predator advances,
His tiny little chest clenches as he waits,
But then . . . he is hit.
The mouse tasted blood,
Arm raised above his head, he squeaked.
'Please, spare me!'
He had asked too much,
Cowering in the corner,
He knew it was the end.

Scott Moir (10)
Crombie Primary School, Westhill

HAPPINESS

Happiness tastes like vanilla ice cream
Happiness smells like a Subaru seat
Happiness looks like the fun of children playing in the park
Happiness sounds like glittery red fireworks.

Gregor Morrice (10)
Crombie Primary School, Westhill

EXCITEMENT

Excitement's the colour of a rainbow
Shining brightly in the sky,
It tastes like fresh bacon and eggs,
Excitement smells of the fresh meadow.
On a summer morning,
It looks like the bright flowers
Dancing in the fresh spring breeze,
Excitement sounds like the birds singing in the morning
And it feels like the soft sand of Bermuda
Flowing through my hands,
Excitement feels good.

Nicole Beedie (10)
Crombie Primary School, Westhill

FEAR

Fear is as black as the darkest night,
It tastes like uncooked chicken,
It smells like the blood dripping from the ceiling,
Fear looks like the fire roaming towards me,
It sounds like the scariest scream,
Fear feels like the scariest man controlling the night storm,
It feels like the tarantulas crawling on my feet,
Fear is the dead spirits burning my body,
Fear is the thought of my dying, unexpectedly.

Ewan Diack (11)
Crombie Primary School, Westhill

Fear

Fear is black like the dripping oil,
It tastes like black burnt toast,
It smells like the old, old sock down the back of the sofa,
It looks like the coal burning in the fire,
It sounds like footsteps thumping up the stairs,
It feels like detention on a summer's day.

Caroline Will (10)
Crombie Primary School, Westhill

Happiness

Happiness is bright yellow like the sun shining
It tastes like strawberries and cream,
Happiness smells like the freshness of freshly grown flowers,
It looks like newly born puppies,
It sounds like people laughing,
It feels like sand running through your hands.

Verity Clark (10)
Crombie Primary School, Westhill

Love Is . . .

Pink as the colour of heart,
It tastes like strawberries and cream,
It smells like pink roses,
It looks like a house of roses,
It sounds like a fizzing bath bomb,
Love feels fluffy like a pussy cat.

Hayley Brown (10)
Crombie Primary School, Westhill

HAPPINESS

Happiness is yellow like the bright sun
Happiness tastes like a sweet lollipop
Happiness smells like a lovely beautiful flower
It sounds like children laughing
It looks like a small, cute puppy dog barking
Happiness feels as relaxing as a nice warm bath.

Andrew Coates (10)
Crombie Primary School, Westhill

THE GYMNASTIC COMPETITION

I'm just entering the gym,
I want my team to win,
I'm getting changed,
The teams are arranged,
I wish my turn was over!

We're getting in line,
I'm feeling just fine,
My turn has come,
I wish I could run,
I wish my turn was over!

The presentation is here,
I'm hearing a cheer,
I've had really good fun,
I've actually won,
I'm glad that my turn is over!

Megan Quinn (10)
Culter Primary School, Peterculter

THEY WERE EASY AND SLOW

They were easy and slow
They're the easiest ever foe
It was 3-0
They started writing their will
It's good we won the game!

I came on in the second half
And then made a superb pass
I scored!
Their defenders snored
It's good we won the game!

They thought we were ace
You should have seen our pace!
We shook their hands
And cheered all our fans
It's good we won the game!

Joanne Murphy (10)
Culter Primary School, Peterculter

GHOSTS

G hosts are such creepy things
H aunting you during the night
O n full moon nights
S inging haunted songs
T hey give you such a fright
S pooky creatures please leave
Is it me or is it shadows that I see?

Sean McFarlane (10)
Culter Primary School, Peterculter

I Wish I Could Be More Fit!

I do a handstand then fall over,
Try a cartwheel and land on my shoulder,
Afterwards my body is sore,
I feel I'm going to collapse on the floor,
I wish I could be more fit.

I kick a ball and trip,
I can't even jump or skip,
Turning around, my head's in a spin,
I've fallen again and hurt my shin,
I wish I could be more fit.

Running around,
Falling to the ground,
Now I'm covered in bumps,
All you see is lumps,
I wish I could be more fit.

Jorja Anderson (10)
Culter Primary School, Peterculter

Snowing

S lipping, sliding, sledging down a hill
N o sun to be seen
O llying down the hill too
W eaving in and out of snow and ramps
I cy roads and icicles hanging from roofs
N aughty people throwing snowballs!
G liding skiers, skaters, snowboards and a sledge.

William McKay (11)
Culter Primary School, Peterculter

THE FOOTBALL MATCH

They're 5-0 up
And they're scoring fast,
They're big and strong
And they're running past,
I wish we could win the game.

We're still losing
And they're bored,
We're losing the ball
And they've scored,
I wish we could win the game.

They've won the match
And we've lost the game,
They're celebrating
And it's such a shame,
I wish we'd won the game!

Liam Shaw (11)
Culter Primary School, Peterculter

NATURE'S WONDER

B ig, beautiful butterfly
U p, up, up it goes
T iny as a caterpillar
T ight in that little cocoon
E ager to escape
R elief it's in the air
F lying, fluttering in the blue sky
L onging to spread its wings
Y ellow, blue and amber, that beautiful butterfly.

Sandra Stewart (10)
Culter Primary School, Peterculter

I Wish I Had A Dog

I love dogs, I think they're the best,
They are better than all the rest,
One bad thing is when they give you a kiss,
Your cheek gets covered with slobberiness,
I wish I had a dog.

I would like a dog, I would call him Rover,
I would teach him to sit and roll over,
I would make sure he gets his food,
So he would never be in a mood,
I wish I had a dog.

I would give him a big, white bone
And I would never leave him on his own,
I would play with him every day,
Rover and I would always play,
I wish I had a dog.

Dailin Hope (10)
Culter Primary School, Peterculter

The Boy Called Lot

There once was a boy called Lot,
Whose nose had a very big spot,
His hooter was red
And his skin half dead,
So the doctor gave him a shot.

Kayleigh Fraser (10)
Culter Primary School, Peterculter

Tiger

The tiger lurks in the long, tall grass,
Waiting for the hare to pass,
The tiger jumps out,
The hare runs about,
Will he catch his prey?

They run around and around,
Chasing without a sound,
The tiger is starting to gain,
The hare is in pain,
Will he catch his prey?

Chasing on the dry, dusty ground,
Then with a rustling sound,
The tiger jumps in the air
And lands on the hare,
He has caught his prey!

Kirsty Donaldson (10)
Culter Primary School, Peterculter

Teddy Bear

A bear is so grizzly and warm
This friend won't do any harm
This little bear is so cuddly and small
If I had him, he will not fall
His favourite food is honey
And all his friends think he is very funny.

Jodie Selfridge (10)
Culter Primary School, Peterculter

Lord Of The Rings

L ord of the Rings is so great
O h the Dark Lord, we'll decide his fate!
R inging blades of clashing swords
D arting arrows of Elven lords

O rcs building armies fast
F alling quickly, they're dead at last

T heoden, King of Rohan high
H ow could he so quickly die?
E ven Elven heroes weep and cry

R oaring battle cries at Helms Deep
I n middle earth life is at risk
N o brave man could ever turn back
G hastly screeching Nazgul brings death
S oon Borimir will take his last breath.

Sacha Christie (10)
Culter Primary School, Peterculter

Limerick

There was an old man from Peru
Who only wore one shoe
One foot was hot
The other was not
So his foot started turning blue.

Keelan Pirie (10)
Culter Primary School, Peterculter

A Heart Of Gold!

Her heart is as big as the world around her,
She could fit everyone inside,
She likes all animals (especially furry ones)
And doesn't judge anything by the outside,
She helps around her city,
Her family helps around too,
She thinks everyone is witty
And she has a part-time job at the zoo,
She helps people when they're hurt
And gives them a plaster or a wet rag
When they've fallen in the dirt,
She'll be there with everything in a bag,
On Sundays she works at a nursing home
And helps the old ladies with their hair,
They put on their coats without a moan
And she takes them out into the fresh air.

Carla England (11)
Culter Primary School, Peterculter

Snowball

S now is real fun but it is very cold
N oisy people are the best, but playing in snow is much better
O nly snow is the best thing in the world
W indy, winter, cold weather isn't nice unless it brings snow
B alls are made to make snowmen and make angels too
A ll winter people would wear gloves and scarves and much more
L ast into school because the snow slows everything down
L ittle people and big people like the snow too!

Jamie Stroud (10)
Culter Primary School, Peterculter

My Fears

This will be about my fears
And where and when I shed a tear,
I toss and turn every night,
Because every dream gives me a fright,
I wish I wasn't a scaredy cat.

Sounds scare me too,
Bangs, clangs and moos,
Rattling, clattering, all day and night
And every time they give me a fright,
I wish I wasn't a scaredy cat.

Gnomes and trolls,
Witches with moles,
They say they're pretend,
But for me it won't end,
I'm still a scaredy cat.

Jennifer Robb (10)
Culter Primary School, Peterculter

Limerick

There once was a man from Japan
Who got hit on the head with a pan
He fell on his face
Saw stars like in space
That poor little man from Japan.

Mark Smith (10)
Culter Primary School, Peterculter

The Animal Race

Birds flutter,
Mice scutter,
The foxes are fast,
But the snails are going to be last,
Who is going to be first?

The squirrel is in the lead,
But the racoon is gaining speed,
The mice are on the run,
They're all having such fun,
Who is going to be first?

The badger has passed the fox,
But the fox is hot on his socks,
The line is in sight,
They will have to put up a fight,
Who is going to be first?

Nikki Cunningham (10)
Culter Primary School, Peterculter

Brothers

B rothers are mean
R ough and tough
O ut of this world
T oy with your brain
H ave such a laugh at you!
E ntering your room
R avaging through your stuff
S o that's what they're like!

Natalie Robb (10)
Culter Primary School, Peterculter

The Big Cat And The Little Mouse

Once a little mouse
Was going to his house,
But a cat as vicious as could be
Attacked him and the mouse said, 'Deary me!

Oh drat! I don't want to be eaten by this cat.'

The cat sprang and the chase was on,
They ran until they were on the lawn,
The cat pounced with its sharp teeth,
The poor mouse yelled, 'Good grief!

Oh drat, I'm going to be eaten by this cat!'

The big fat cat licked its lips,
The mouse had sadly had its chips,
As the great pussy said, 'Yummy!'
A voice came from inside its tummy!

'Oh drat! I was eaten by this cat!'

Euan Ferguson (10)
Culter Primary School, Peterculter

CYCLING

I like to ride my bike,
But not with Mike,
He comes with me everywhere,
We go here and there,
I wish he didn't have to come.

We go down to the river,
Mike starts to shiver,
We stop for a snack,
Mike starts to pack,
I wish he didn't have to come.

I can cycle up a hill,
But Mike will,
Only cycle halfway up,
While I am drinking 7UP,
I'm not taking him with me again!

Leanne Christie (10)
Culter Primary School, Peterculter

Winning Chess

I'm beating the best,
He's better than the rest,
I don't know how,
But I'm beating him now,
I'm going to win the game!

He's tearing out his hair,
I don't think he can bear,
That in school I'll be a saint,
I think I'm going to faint!
I'm going to win the game!

I've taken his queen,
His face is turning green,
He's worried for his fate,
Oh look! It's checkmate!
I've finally won the game!

Matthew Kidd (11)
Culter Primary School, Peterculter

TESTS

I'm sitting in the classroom doing a test,
The teacher said to do our best,
But I'm not,
I don't know what to do.
I don't have a clue,
I hope I pass this test!

I still don't know what to do,
Maybe I should pretend that I have the flu,
I really want to go home,
I want to give out a loud groan,
I hope I pass this test!

Later on in May,
I got a letter about that day,
It was good enough to pass,
I felt like a happy lass,
I'm glad I passed that test!

Somhairle Cruickshank (10)
Culter Primary School, Peterculter

THE FOOTBALL GAME

They're a stronger team than us,
We're missing out top goalie, Russ,
They take a shot at goal,
It goes in with a roll,
I wish we could win the game.

We give them a foul,
They start to growl,
Our team is a mess,
They are winning I guess,
I wish we could win the game.

There is five minutes to go,
The ref is going to blow,
A chance for a goal!
The ball hits the pole!
I wish we had won the game.

Ewan McRae (10)
Culter Primary School, Peterculter

The Test

I am sitting in the classroom
Doing a test
The teacher said to do our best
But I am not
I wish this test would end!

I am watching the clock go *tick-tock*
Every second
Every minute
Go by
I wish this test would end!

It's almost time to stop
I can hear the clock
Oh no
Oh no
I haven't even started!

Nicole Ross (10)
Culter Primary School, Peterculter

SWINGING ON MY CHAIR

I walk into that dreaded room,
I'm about to make myself look like a spoon,
I begin to rock on my chair,
It gets much worse from there,
I know I shouldn't do this.

I swung on my chair
And flew through the air,
Landed on the floor,
Very near the door,
I wish I hadn't done that!

As I landed I hit my head,
I really thought that I was dead!
It felt as if the bump on my head
Was the size of a double bed,
I wish I hadn't done that!

I woke up in casualty,
Beside people with worse injuries than me,
My head was throbbing,
My eyes were bobbing,
I wish I hadn't done that!

The doctor said I'd be OK,
But I had to stay in for a couple of days,
I've learned my lesson,
I've changed my ways,
I won't swing on a chair again!

Jordan Sparrow (10)
Culter Primary School, Peterculter

CHRISTMAS

It's as big as a huge present waiting to be opened
And as small as a white mouse sheltering from the snow.

It's as loud as carol singers chanting all kinds of
different Christmas songs
And as quiet as glittering snow falling from the sky.

It's as colourful as brightly coloured lights twinkling on the window
And as dull as a striped suit made out of wool.

It's as jolly as red cheeked Santa filling the sleigh with presents
And as tasty as stuffed chicken cooking in the oven.

It's all these things you see
Is what Christmas means to me!

Sarah Mills (10)
East End Primary School, Elgin

CHRISTMAS

It's as cold as dripping icicles stuck upon a roof
And as hot as a burning fire with my feet beside it.

It's as tasty as a delicious turkey sitting on a dinner table
And as soft as baby Jesus rocking in his cosy cradle.

It's as jolly as fat old Santa laughing with happiness
And as noisy as bursting crackers exploding at a Christmas party.

It's as quiet as a falling snowflake from the sky
And as beautiful as a sparkly angel on top of the Christmas tree.

It's all the things you see
But it's not spring, it's Christmas.

Claire Grant (10)
East End Primary School, Elgin

CHRISTMAS

It's as quiet as a falling snowflake drifting from a sheet of white snow
And as loud as an exploding cracker at a Christmas party.

It's as fat as jolly Santa rolling down a hill
And as thin as a squeezing elf trying to get down a chimney.

It's as big as a tall Christmas tree in a room lit up with lights
And as small as a baby lamb sleeping quietly in a barn.

It's as red as Rudolph's nose shining in the black sky
And as black as the night's sky where Santa rides his sleigh.

It's all these things that you see
It's what Christmas means to me.

Duncan Innes (10)
East End Primary School, Elgin

CHRISTMAS CONUNDRUM

It's as cold as shivering white snow covering the land as it
reaches the ground
And as warm as a blazing hot fire heating up the room.

It's as boring as a big pair of woolly socks you're giving your dad
And as exciting as a brilliant toy you've been waiting for.

It's as quiet as a crying field mouse hiding from a blizzard
And as loud as fat Santa shouting for help when he's stuck
in the chimney.

It's as happy as jolly children playing in the snow
And as shiny as a star in the midnight sky.

It's all these things you see,
Because it's not a monster - it's Christmas!

Ian Thomson (10)
East End Primary School, Elgin

CHRISTMAS

It's as fat as laughing Santa coming down the chimney
And as glittery as falling snow drifting from the sky.
It's as sparkly as colourful tinsel glowing in the light.
It's as quiet as all the children waiting to go down the stairs
And as loud as all the noisy children pulling the Christmas cracker.
It's as shimmery as the beautiful fairy sitting at the top of the tree
And as glowing as all the candles lighting up the rooms.
It's as tasty as all the food on the table waiting to be eaten.
It's all these things you see
It's what Christmas means to me.

Ashleigh Grant (10)
East End Primary School, Elgin

CHRISTMAS

It's as quiet as a falling snowflake floating down from the
blanket-like sky
And as loud as a booming cracker at the Christmas party.
It's as white as a baby lamb sitting in the barn
And as red as Rudolph's nose shining in the pitch-black sky.
It's as tall as the Christmas tree reaching to the roof with
lovely decorations
And as shiny as sparkly tinsel hanging off the decorated tree.
It's as jolly as Santa laughing through the night and squeezing
through the chimney
And as joyful as carol singers singing in the street.
It's all the things you can see
Is what Christmas means to me.

Calum Leiper (10)
East End Primary School, Elgin

CHRISTMAS

It's as quick as a falling snowflake gentle drifting to the ground
And as loud as a banging cracker being pulled at Christmas parties.

It's as big as a huge colourful parcel waiting to be opened
And as beautiful as sparkling decorations hung around the room.

It's as white as sparkling white snow lying on the ground
And as black as the night sky which Santa rides through.

It's as jolly as laughing Santa coming down the chimney
And as excited as patient children waiting to open parcels.

It's all these things you see
This is what Christmas means to me.

Lauren Ford (10)
East End Primary School, Elgin

CHRISTMAS

It's as soft as children singing carols in the street
And as loud as a banging popper at a party.

It's as hot as a roasting turkey in the oven
And as cold as shimmering snow falling from the sky.

It's as dark as the night sky on Christmas Eve
And as light as a massive Christmas tree.

It's as excited as my little brother running downstairs
And as calm as a baby lamb lying in the barn.

Stewart McLaren (10)
East End Primary School, Elgin

CHRISTMAS

It's as quiet as a falling snowflake drifting gently from the night sky
And as noisy as a popping popper banging the night away.

It's as magical as Santa's reindeer trotting along swiftly
through the night
And as red as Rudolph's nose glistening in the moonlight.

It's as happy as jolly Santa laughing and chuckling away
And as excited as chatting adults waiting for joyful presents.

It's as cold as a winter night whistling gently in the glowing window
And as hungry as bursting children eating till their heart's content.

It's all these things to me
It's Christmas - it's a simile!

Hannah Scott (10)
East End Primary School, Elgin

CHRISTMAS

It's as quiet as Santa slipping down the chimney
And as loud as Santa falling on to the floor.
It's as beautiful as the angel glittering on top of the tree
And as ugly as Jack Frost making it freezing cold.
It's as busy as elves rushing to get everything ready
And as lazy as Rudolph arguing with Santa that it is too cold to go.
It's as happy as children opening their presents
And as sad as elves sobbing that they're not getting paid
for another year.

All these things put together makes
A brilliant Christmas for me!

Georgia Stewart (11)
East End Primary School, Elgin

CHRISTMAS

It's as yummy as a chocolate pudding waiting to be eaten
And as horrible as a greasy turkey getting passed around the table.

It's as noisy as screaming carol singers singing their hymns
And as quiet as a falling snowflake glistening in the sky.

It's as cold as white ice shivering up your back
And as hot as the burning fire lighting up the moon.

It's as jolly as fat Santa sliding down your chimney
And as sad as little children that don't get any presents at all.

It's all these things you see
That's what Christmas means to me!

Stacey Jackson (10)
East End Primary School, Elgin

CHRISTMAS

It's as cold as the shimmering snow falling gently from the sky
And as hot as steaming Christmas pudding looking too good to eat.

It's as loud as singing carollers reaching high pitched notes
And as quiet as a mouse scampering around the beautiful tree.

It's as colourful as dangling decorations glimmering on the tree
And as shiny as tinsel hanging off the wall.

It's as fat as jolly Santa going down the chimney
And as tasty as stuffed turkey waiting to be eaten.

That's what Christmas means to me.

Callum Watson (10)
East End Primary School, Elgin

CAPTURE

I want to capture the sound of the East End choir singing
their lovely songs.
I want to capture the feel of silk rubbing against my hand.
I want to capture the smell of pizza coming out of the oven.
I want to capture the sight of the waves crashing against the rocks.
I want to capture the taste of my mum's delicious cooking.
I want to capture the moment when my baby cousin was born.
I want to capture the memory of my friends when I leave
East End Primary.
I want to capture the silence of my house when everyone is asleep.
I want to capture the feeling I get when I am happy and keep it
with me forever.

Joe Williams (11)
East End Primary School, Elgin

A RECIPE FOR CHRISTMAS

Take a handful of sparkling ice-cold snow
And a tall green Christmas tree with its coloured lights.
Mix in the excitement you feel on Christmas Eve
As you wonder what presents you will get.
Add the smell of the tasty, crispy turkey
Cooking lightly in the warm oven.
Bake for a month in the light of the glistening silver stars.
Now you have made the perfect Christmas of all.

Zara-Ann McKenzie (11)
East End Primary School, Elgin

CAPTURE

I want to capture the sound of an owl hooting in the trees.
I want to capture the feel of silk rubbing against my skin.
I want to capture the smell of a chicken roasting in the oven.
I want to capture the sight of the sea smashing against the rocks.
I want to capture the taste of Yorkshire puddings crunching
in my mouth.
I want to capture the moment when my baby brother was born.
I want to capture the memory of when I first came to
East End Primary.
I want to capture the silence when everybody is sleeping at night.
I want to capture the feeling of happiness when my family
go on holiday.

Steven Lyons (11)
East End Primary School, Elgin

CHRISTMAS

It's as colourful as Santa's sledge sparkling, glittering in the
black night sky
And as white as an angel's wings sparkling on my tall tree.
It's as red as Rudolph's nose flashing in the pitch black
And as loud as a bursting cracker exploding at a Christmas party.
It's all the things you can see
It's what Christmas means to me!

Allan Slapp (10)
East End Primary School, Elgin

CHRISTMAS POEM

It's as cold as a dancing snowflake twisting around and around
And as jolly as Santa placing presents in stockings.

It's like excited children going to open presents
And as a huge present waiting to be opened.

It's as stuffed as a stocking laid gently on the seat
And as big as a long table full of a steaming Christmas feast.

It's Jesus' birthday now
And that's what Christmas means to me.

Steven Webster (10)
East End Primary School, Elgin

A CHRISTMAS SPECIAL

It's as bright as a flickering fire blowing warmth around the house
And as still as icicles hanging from the rooftop.
It's as hot as a juicy, crisp turkey sitting on the table
And as cold as the freezing snowflakes falling from the sky.
It's as happy as the chilly Christmas carollers wandering the streets
And as upset as sad people remembering their dead family.
You make Christmas beautiful in a simile
It's as graceful as a glittering angel sitting on the Christmas tree
And as a gleaming Christmas tree with tinsel and lights.

Staci Smith (10)
East End Primary School, Elgin

CAPTURE

I want to capture the sound of my mum singing in the house.
I want to capture the feel of my baby brother's soft skin.
I want to capture the smell of cakes cooking in the warm oven.
I want to capture the sight of the sun shining high up in the sky.
I want to capture the taste of my mum's delicious cooking.
I want to capture the moment when my baby brother was born
and was wrapped in a warm blanket.
I want to capture the memory of Primary 5 when I went into the
classroom and met my new teacher.
I want to capture the silence of the snow falling to the ground.
I want to capture the feeling I get when my mum smiles at me
when I am sad.

Lauren Hambly (11)
East End Primary School, Elgin

CAPTURE

I want to capture the sound of people playing at the park.
I want to capture the feel of my woollen scarf around my neck.
I want to capture the smell of my Christmas dinner cooking in the oven.
I want to capture the sight of the sun going down after a busy day.
I want to capture the taste of cheese melting in my mouth.
I want to capture the moment when I first started playgroup.
I want to capture the memory of my first term in Primary 1.
I want to capture the silence in my class when everyone is
working hard.
I want to capture the feeling of excitement when it is Christmas.

Gemma-Louise Taylor (11)
East End Primary School, Elgin

CAPTURE

I want to capture the sound of hailstones bouncing off my umbrella.
I want to capture the feel of my cat's fluffy hair on my skin.
I want to capture the smell of food cooking in a restaurant.
I want to capture the sight of the sun setting after a hot busy day.
I want to capture the taste of macaroni cheese as this is
my favourite meal.
I want to capture the moment when I first saw my mum and dad
So I can look back and see what they looked like then.
I want to capture the memory of my great granny's smile.
I want to capture the silence of my house when my family and I
go to bed at night.
I want to capture the feeling of happiness and lock it in a box
and open it whenever I feel sad.

Claire Sutherland (12)
East End Primary School, Elgin

CAPTURE

I want to capture the sound of a wolf howling in the night.
I want to capture the feel of grass against my skin.
I want to capture the smell of bacon sizzling in the microwave.
I want to capture the sight of happy people playing in the park.
I want to capture the taste of Chinese food in my mouth.
I want to capture the memory of the day I started school.
I want to capture the silence of the calm sea.
I want to capture the feeling of happiness and joy.

Michael Paterson (11)
East End Primary School, Elgin

CAPTURE

I want to capture the sound of people cheering me on at football.
I want to capture the feel of my cats when they are up close beside me.
I want to capture the smell of my Sunday dinner cooking in the oven.
I want to capture the sight of Blackpool from its huge tower.
I want to capture the taste of gravy sliding down my throat.
I want to capture the moment when my granda walked out after
his dangerous operation.
I want to capture the memory of meeting my great, great granny
because I've only met her once.
I want to capture the silence in my house when we are in our beds.
I want to capture the feeling of happiness,
Hide it in a box and take it out when I am sad.

Andrew Jackson (12)
East End Primary School, Elgin

A RECIPE FOR CHRISTMAS

Take Rudolph's lovely bright red nose
And add a little piece of tinsel sparkling like a diamond.
Stir in some glistening cold snow
And excited children building snowmen.
Mix in a six foot fir tree with lovely coloured lights
And lots of beautiful decorations.
Add a delicious chocolate Advent calendar
And lots of big colourful presents.
Finally, add a helping of mouth-watering turkey
Leave in an ice-cold breeze for one month
And you have made a brilliant Christmas.

Kenneth Greaves (11)
East End Primary School, Elgin

A Recipe For Christmas

Take the sound of Santa and his reindeer landing on the roof
And mix that with the lovely gifts he leaves.
Stir in some juicy turkey covered with gravy
And Christmas pudding smothered in cream.
Mix in the crackers that you open with your family and friends
Then the delicious chocolates that are hanging from the tall
green Christmas tree.
Add in all the grateful people who are saying thanks for all their
spectacular gifts.
Finally, add the lovely snowman that the children worked hard to make,
Now you can enjoy the best Christmas ever.

Ross Archibald (11)
East End Primary School, Elgin

Capture

I want to capture the sound of people arguing and lock it away forever.
I want to capture the feel of a cashmere scarf rubbing against my neck.
I want to capture the smell of toast burning in the toaster.
I want to capture the sight of the sun reflecting off the sea.
I want to capture the taste of butter melting in my mouth.
I want to capture the moment when I got my first bike for Christmas.
I want to capture the memory of my first day at East End School.
I want to capture the silence in the streets when everyone's asleep.
I want to capture the feeling of happiness when I go away on holiday.

Jamie-Ann Docherty (11)
East End Primary School, Elgin

It Could Have Been . . .

Last night I heard a sound,
It could have been a mouse squeaking under my bed.
It could have been an owl hooting in the trees.
It could have been my cat screeching at next door's dog.
It could have been the heavy rain hitting against my window.
It could have been a ghost roaming through my house,
But it was only my dad snoring like a monster!

Liam Archibald (11)
East End Primary School, Elgin

War!

War is full of anger, rage and terror,
Scaring many people and children all over the world.
On moonlit nights, so quiet, like a baby fast asleep in a blanket,
Then *bang* as loud as a bomb, hitting a skyscraper.
Little babies screaming in their beds
And mothers running as fast as wind to calm them down.
Fathers working in factories, making all the machinery used in the war.
Young boys, preparing to go to war, as scared as being in a bag
With a very poisonous snake.
Grandmothers and grandfathers working as hard as slaves in a castle,
Just to make money to raise their families.
People want to know *why war?* What have we done?
But they don't get an answer.
Germans planning to kill or how to run the concentration camps,
When Jews are planning how to get out.
They are rushed into showers as fast as cattle moving through fields
And then, death.
The Germans are doing this just to get money.
Nobody has time to stand and stare.

Stephanie Asher (10)
Foveran Primary School, Foveran

WAR!

Unhappy, angry children are taken away from their loving families
And evacuated to the country.
Planes screech over the top of the rooftops as the bombs start to fall,
Sending fires blazing around the town, spreading like a virus.
Bombs falling from the sky like heavy, stormy rain showers.
Tanks roaring through the cities striking fear in innocent
people's hearts.
Grenades going off here and there, killing helpless, innocent people.
Deserted towns crumbling, people suffer from constant bombing raids.
Unhappiness all around as people search for their surviving
friends and families.

Sarah Buchan & Norman Campbell (11)
Foveran Primary School, Foveran

WAR

War is like a bolt of lightning, it's so very sharp.
The tank's caterpillar tread slips in the mud
Like a snake going through long grass.
Warships thrusting through the sea
Like deadly sea monsters.
German U-boats deadly like water snakes.
Death coming like a ship's radar sweeping over the world.
Planes buzzing like bees flying over the world.
Adolf Hitler dictating Germany,
A one man force.
Mud on the battlefield like slimy glue.

Johnathan Kain (9)
Foveran Primary School, Foveran

WAR!

War is a deadly plague destroying families.
Bombs explode much like eggs in pans, hitting buildings and boats.
Death, terror as well as fear is shooting into hearts,
Like bolts of lightning.
Destruction like a Lego town being stood on by a baby brother.
Guns go off like a sudden smash of two cars colliding with each other
As the air bags inflate like balloons,
Sounds of the smashing and crashing,
Like a bull in a china shop.
The noise is similar to a room of thirty children screeching and crying.
Warships sinking like a ton of stones being dumped into a lake.
Zoom go the planes like a dreamy boy in the playground who thinks
He is a pilot of a war plane.
The rush of the shock struck civilians during a bomb raid
Reminds me of a bullet out of a gun.
The bright moon is like a lighthouse giving sight for all this plague.

Ryan Bennett (10)
Foveran Primary School, Foveran

WAR!

War is coming,
The submarines dive,
The bombs fall
And the children cry,
Women scream,
Men shout,
Planes zoom overhead,
People lie in bed,
As still as death.

Kathryn Cruickshank (10)
Foveran Primary School, Foveran

War!

War is loud, scary with black bombs
Thumping on the ground like elephants.
War is frightening, sad and upsetting.
Planes rushing through the sky like a bullet out of a gun.
Dark, lonely streets on a moonlight night,
Everyone in their shelters like foxes in a den.
Innocent people fighting for their lives in the war.
Unhappy people in their houses,
Babies crying as loud as a door banging.
Soldiers stuck in the trenches, wanting to go home.
Soldiers cold, wet, smelly and lonely in the sloppy, squelchy mud.
Bombs dropping from the sky like a bird swooping for his prey,
Bang! The town is destroyed, lit up with flames.
Exploding torpedoes from U-boats moving like hot,
Sizzling, banging sausages.

Nicola Buchan (9)
Foveran Primary School, Foveran

War

War in the trenches is terrifying.
Men squelching in the cold sloppy mud,
Grenades exploding all around them.
Soldiers are running fast trying to escape danger.
Sounds, the rapid fire of the guns were very loud.
Tanks roaring, guns ready to fire.
Planes in the sky were laden with bombs,
They were going to Germany to cause destruction.
Carriers out in the ocean, looking for a target.
Depth-charges loaded ready to blow up
German U-boats.

Stephen Nightingale (9)
Foveran Primary School, Foveran

War!

War, like a raging, angry eruption,
Bombs, loud as thunder, never stopping.
Tanks going *bang, bang, bang*, day and night like tigers roaring,
Warships on the water crashing through the waves
And shooting other warships and it's loud
And dangerous like monkeys that roar and lions that eat you alive,
Planes letting out the rage of bombs
Like rats scuttling through the house and letting off a smell,
Life of people being made to death like a bug had been squashed,
Boys wanting to fight in the war
Like snakes forcing a bird egg down its throat,
Destruction of houses by the bombs and people falling to the ground
Like many trees falling at the same time.
Guns being shot furiously like a bad blizzard
Grenades being thrown towards soldiers and innocent people,
Like a boomerang being thrown at an animal.
Mud being splashed around as people run to escape the guns
Like running in a game of tig and tag.
Armies marching in line training for the war like a pack of wolves
Trying to kill two people.

Iona McLeod (10)
Foveran Primary School, Foveran

Exercise

Exercise, exercise, any form of exercise
Cycling and walking are good for you
Swimming and roller-skating are fun
So do yourself some good
And do some exercise.

Harry Reeder (9)
Fyvie Primary School, Turriff

Pop Stars

Pop stars, pop stars stuck on my wall,
Darius is great and he's six feet tall.

Eminem the rapper, he's totally cool,
What about David, his songs rule.

Busted, Busted they are the best,
Avril is better than all the rest.

Can't forget Ms Dynamite, she is the queen,
Girls Aloud they make a good team.

Venessa Carlton with Counting Crows,
Justin knows everything Geri knows.

That's my list of the greatest stars,
Even better, they've got great flashy cars.

Kirsten Gall (10)
Fyvie Primary School, Turriff

If It Is A Sunny Day

If it is a sunny day,
I would go out and play.

If it is a sunny day,
I would play with my bunny.

If it is a sunny day,
I might have a rumbly tummy.

Fiona Crawford (9)
Fyvie Primary School, Turriff

What If?

What if it was sunny?
Would I play with my bunny?

What if it was raining?
Would I be complaining?

What if it was snowing?
Would the wind be blowing?

What if it started to hail?
Would I turn pale?

What if there was a hurricane?
Would the world come to an end?

Emily England (8)
Fyvie Primary School, Turriff

Myself

I think to myself in my strange little mind
and I think it over again.

For my mother has said over tea,
'Jam and bread, what a strange little girl I am.'

Why am I strange? What makes me so weird?
What kind of girl must I be?

So I think to myself in my strange little mind
and I think it over again.

Mary Heaton (10)
Fyvie Primary School, Turriff

MOTOR RACING

M otor racing, motor racing, going very fast
O n and off the road, will it ever last?
T oday and tomorrow, will it ever last?
O ther people think I'm crazy, I wish to be a racer
R acers get loads of money, then I'll be rich

R eally other people think I'm crazy because I called my mum a witch
A person I know is really good at racing
C an this person join the race? His wish is to be a racer
I t's really thirsty work, do they ever get to stop?
N ow ready to race
G oing on and off the road, I hope it will stop.

Arran Donald (11)
Fyvie Primary School, Turriff

MOTOCROSS

M otorbikes revving their engines
O ver the jump doing a no-hander lander
T ime is running out to get in first place
O ther bikes spraying mud everywhere
C urving round the corner nearly falling off
R evving engines, nearly overheating
O ver the hill, coming to the finish line
S liding past the other bikes, shouting, 'Slow coaches!'
S itting on the seat and rolling past the finish line.

Martyn Black (11)
Fyvie Primary School, Turriff

DANCE!

Dance, dance
I love to dance
I prance and prance
Until I'm in a trance
I jive, jive and I'm never deprived
Dancing is my world

Boogie, boogie
Get on down
As the CD in the player
Goes round and round

Break, tap, jazz
Hip hop, street
Contemporary and ballet
They'll all get you on your feet

So dance, dance
I love to dance
Dancing is my world.

Sophie McWilliam (11)
Fyvie Primary School, Turriff

THE CROCODILES

The crocodiles jump and turn into lumps
And they splash and crash
And when it's dinner time
Snap, snap.

Philip Woodward (9)
Fyvie Primary School, Turriff

Rock Star

The rock star
Jumps like mad
Rocks like mad
Thinks mad!

The rock star
Wears baggy clothes
Weird clothes
Odd clothes
Black clothes

The rock star
Has a guitar
A black guitar
A new guitar

The rock star
Jumps cool
Walks cool
Talks cool
Sings cool.

Marion Fisher (10)
Fyvie Primary School, Turriff

Beaver Weaver

Beavers are good weavers
When it comes to a dam
Beavers are good weavers
Even on land
But beavers aren't good weavers
When they see a man.

Robbie Faquhar (9)
Fyvie Primary School, Turriff

My Friend

My friend is always there for me,
When I was sad, she filled me with glee,
Someone to care about who cares about me,
I never knew what a good friend she'd be.

When she first came here, I thought she was bad,
But then it turned out she was just sad,
Once I got to know her, I was glad,
The best friend I ever had!

When she left, tears rolled down my cheek,
I looked as though I'd sprung a leak,
But now I see her every week
And together we watch Dawson's Creek!

Lyndsay Mackie (10)
Fyvie Primary School, Turriff

My Pet Cat

When my pet cat is annoyed
She bites and scratches
And when you try to pet her
Then she growls and hisses

When my pet cat is hungry
She miaows in the kitchen
And when she is eating
Then she purrs and purrs

When my pet cat is playing
With her little ball
Then she chases when I throw it
She runs very fast.

William Wilson (11)
Fyvie Primary School, Turriff

I Had A Best Friend

I had a best friend
To talk to at school,
She was the best,
She really did rule.

I had a best friend
To play with at home
And when I went away,
I felt all alone.

I had a best friend
To write to each week,
She brightened me up,
When life was bleak.

I had a best friend,
But not every day,
Now I have a new friend
To talk to at play.

Caroline Esslemont (10)
Fyvie Primary School, Turriff

Aberdeen Town

Busy town, cars brimming around,
Traffic jams and people rushing around in their cars,
To get to their work in their cars,
Boats in the sea and oil rigs spilling their oil
And killing the fishes.

Aidan Hutcheon (9)
Fyvie Primary School, Turriff

SUPERSTAR

Galloping down the field,
Sleeping in the stable,
Eating its food,
But it's no good,
Fat she is,
Leading my pony,
Around the field,
I jump on her bare back,
Away she goes,
What a superstar she is,
Slim too,
OK, so she'll eat neeps
Until she's one,
But don't be so glum,
She may be old but
She's my superstar
And my friend!

Holly Johnston (11)
Fyvie Primary School, Turriff

POP STARS

Pop stars are cool
Pop stars are funky
Pop stars have got cool cars
Pop stars have got posh things
Pop stars have got cool songs and dances
Pop stars have got everything.

Monica Crawford (9)
Fyvie Primary School, Turriff

Oops

Wet, wet, wet,
Upstairs, downstairs,
Everything is wet.

Water in the kitchen,
Water on the floor,
Water on the sofa
And water through the door.

Water in my bedroom,
Water everywhere,
Water in the bathroom,
That I really care.

I went to bed too late
And stayed in there too long,
I got up in the morning
And realised I had left
The kitchen tap on!

Gill Christie (11)
Fyvie Primary School, Turriff

Dragons

Dragons are hot, dragons are cold,
Some are young, some are old,
Dragons are white, dragons are red,
Dragons could set fire to your bed,
Dragons breathe ice, dragons breathe fire,
Dragons could melt a thick bit of wire
Dragons have eggs, some have none,
Dragons would hate a big cheese bun.

Ben Bardsley (8)
Fyvie Primary School, Turriff

I Wish

I wish I was a bird
So I could fly high in the sky
And then swoop down
To say hello to birds I know

I wish I had a million bucks
So I could have a pond
With lots of ducks
And to sail my boats along

I wish I could shop all day long
And buy a CD with the greatest song
Then take you out to lunch
And buy you flowers in a big bunch.

Gemma Forbes (11)
Fyvie Primary School, Turriff

The Match

Here comes the ref about to start the match
Here comes the striker flying down the wing
Has time to cross
Here comes the keeper leaping out to catch
The header of Big Bobo
He had no chance!
1-0 to Celtic is the half-time score
Here come the teams, coming out to start
Here comes Larsson to finish off the match
Stops, shoots, scores!
2-0 is the final score, Celtic win!

Gavin Taylor (11)
Fyvie Primary School, Turriff

THE MONSTER

Under the floorboards, under your bed,
Down in the garden, into your shed.

It creeps from the bathroom, up to the loft
And sits on the cushions, ever so soft.

It looms in the darkness, waits for its prey,
It springs out of hiding, it's got food for the day.

Go down in the kitchen and you're certain to see,
This monster in the cupboard, having its tea!

If you are careful and play the right game,
You might catch this monster and may learn his name.

Alex Pithie (11)
Fyvie Primary School, Turriff

RIVER

Water trickles down the stream,
Getting wider and wider, slower and slower,
Slowly turning into the river, wide and long,
Rapids smashing and crashing over stone,
Faster and faster, heading to the waterfall,
Down and down, falling to the bottom of the cliff,
Smashing to the water below
On its way to the sea
The river twists and turns
Coming closer to the sea
Breaking up into small streams
The river reaches the sea and comes to a stop.

Harry Hanson (11)
Fyvie Primary School, Turriff

WIGGLETUMP

He lives in the trash
And loves to *smash, bash* and *crash*
The bottles my mum threw away
I looked in the bin and saw him
All I could do was stare
His big, ugly eyes, his ghostly grin
I better not annoy him.

But then a scream escaped my mouth
He did not stir, he did not move
But then he grabbed my hood
His minky hand wrapped round my neck
I thought, *oh no I'm gonna die*
But then I poked him in the eye
He shrieked and yelled and began to cry
All I said was 'Goodbye.'

The next day I looked in the bin
But I couldn't see him
I rummaged through the bin
But still couldn't see him
A shadow fell over me
Guess who's back? 'It's me!'
The *Wiggletump* grabbed my arm
And I tried to sound an alarm
I hit him right in the head
Then he just fell down dead
He slowly began to disappear
And I was the only one who
Knew he lived here.

Faye Mailley (11)
Fyvie Primary School, Turriff

SEASONS

Winter is the first season
And it's my own favourite,
I love playing in the glistening snow,
But I don't see many birds.

Robins are the birds for winter,
Playing in the snow,
Jumping from tree to tree
And then flying low.

Spring is the second season,
With flowers galore,
Daffodils and bluebells,
More than ever before.

In summer the trees are beautiful,
With lots and lots of flowers,
But then the nasty bees come along
And sting you with their powers.

Autumn leaves fall off the trees
And make huge piles,
Some fall on the grass
And some on the patio tiles.

So winter's my favourite because of the snow,
Second is summer because it's not cold,
Then it is spring with Easter eggs
And last autumn, when leaves cover your legs.

Rebecca Conn (11)
Fyvie Primary School, Turriff

Aberdeen

Aberdeen are the best
Of the rest
Aberdeen can beat
Any other team because
They are the best
Of the rest
So don't mess with
The best because
Aberdeen are the champions
No time for losers because
We are the champions
Of the world.

Sam Wilson (9)
Fyvie Primary School, Turriff

My Pet Dog

My pet dog
He sometimes
Scratches me
But I don't
Really care
Because he
Is fun to
Play with
If I'm sad
He always
Makes me
Really happy
To be there.

Sarah Davidson (11)
Fyvie Primary School, Turriff

Simply Strange

Scaly the croc is a strange croc,
This poem will tell you why,
You know you get normal crocs,
Scary crocs, fat crocs and ugly crocs,
Well, she wears frilly frocks,
She doesn't eat a crocodile's normal food,
But she eats jam roly poly for her pud,
Scaly thinks she is so beautiful,
But if you saw her, you'd be in hysterics,
For she doesn't know how she really looks,
She likes to play Trivial Pursuit and read books,
She's a bit of a sook,
She's just simply strange!

Emily Horn (11)
Fyvie Primary School, Turriff

Liverpool

Liverpool, Liverpool
are simply the best.

They kick the ball
in the back of the net.

That's why Liverpool
are better than all the rest.

Peter Davies (9)
Fyvie Primary School, Turriff

Dundee Derby

Tayside, home to the Arabs
3 o'clock kick-off on the way
Colour disappears as the great
Orange and black seats fill up
The Arabs chanting
As the orange army
Hearts pumping as Dundee United
Wear that famous Dundee United colour
Flags in the air waiting
For the players of Tayside to fill
The pitch for a great game

Dundee fans on the verge to
6th in the SPL
Blue, white and red
Hang on the away side of Tanadice
With scarves and hats.

Janine Gall (11)
Fyvie Primary School, Turriff

My Family

My mum likes cleaning
My dad likes sleeping
My sister likes reading
My cousin likes cheating

My dog likes misbehaving
My cat likes eating
And I don't like speaking.

Sheila Edwards (11)
Fyvie Primary School, Turriff

Dogs

Dogs, dogs, they are cute
And guess what? I've got three,
Holly, Bramble and Bracken too,
They all like to chew my shoe,
Holly is so fluffy, white,
Bramble is lovely in black,
Bracken suits brown and white,
They're all such a delight.

Amy Singer (10)
Fyvie Primary School, Turriff

A Winter World

A cold, dark season,
Filled with white, green and red.
There is a good reason,
To stay in your bed.
Snug and warm like Jesus in the stable,
Linger there as long as you're able.
Snowflakes fall onto the ground,
Some are square and some are round.
Robins tweet perched on a tree,
They are singing merrily.
Frost starts falling on your car,
You keep skidding on the tar.
I just like to stay in bed and
Go to rest my weary head.

Rebekah Wright (12)
Insch Primary School, Insch

Winter, Winter, Wonderful Winter

Winter, winter, wonderful winter
When snow falls, you can see it glinter
Santa's sleigh might give you a splinter

Snow, snow, wonderful snow
It will start to fall when the wind blows
I think Santa's sleigh is ready to go

White, white, wonderful whiteness
Look outside, you just see brightness
Turn on a lamp, it will show the lightness

School, school, when you leave school
Look in your stocking, you just have to drool
The weather of winter is just so cool

Winter, winter, wonderful winter.

Andrew McNamee (11)
Insch Primary School, Insch

On A Cold Frosty Evening

On a cold icy evening
It's hard to walk on an icy road
And an icy path
Ice shines with any type of light
When robins are in your garden in mid autumn
It's a sign that winter's near
Winter is the time of year
When the most accidents happen.

Lee Gillies (11)
Insch Primary School, Insch

This Is What Winter Means To Me

Snow and sleighs
Reindeer and Santa
This is what winter means to me
But don't forget the birth of Jesus

Bells and holly
Angels and cake
This is what winter means to me
But don't forget the birth of Jesus

The colour of white
Snowdrops and snowflakes
This is what winter means to me
But don't forget the birth of Jesus

Advent and gloves
And woolly hats
This is what winter means to me
But don't forget the birth of Jesus

Presents and cold
Snowflakes and snowmen
This is what winter means to me
But don't forget the birth of Jesus.

Jennifer Simpson (11)
Insch Primary School, Insch

That Snowflake

That snowflake falling on my nose,
All the children playing outside in the snow,
Hats and gloves,
Birds like doves.

That snowflake falling on my nose,
The next door neighbour chatting away,
While I stay inside to watch,
Skiers glide.

That snowflake falling on my nose,
Been outside, come back in,
Have some hot chocolate,
Robin redbreast, my best mate.

That snowflake falling on my nose,
Snowballs and snow fights,
Snowdrops and snowflakes,
Snowmen and snow angels,
That snowflake falling on my nose.

Lucy Rowe (11)
Insch Primary School, Insch

Winter Games

A snowy ground
An icy wind
It is coming up to Christmas
Everybody's making snowmen
And playing on the ice
The snowy hills are great to sledge on
Making snow angels is fun
And everybody's happy
Children are having a snowball fight
It looks very enjoyable
And everybody's gloves are soaking
With the icy, wet snow in their hands
Snowflakes begin to fall
Like lacy webs, whirling and twirling
Everybody runs inside
Eyes shining, noses glowing
As I look outside
I see a new blanket of snow forming
With no footprints
It is beautiful.

Eilidh Leask (11)
Insch Primary School, Insch

Christmas Happiness

The first snowflakes are falling,
And the children are calling,
They're happy, jolly and merry!
They're wrapping up warm,
Because of the storm,
They're happy, jolly and merry!
Their laughter is ringing in my ears,
The adults shout, 'Cheers!'
They're happy, jolly and merry!
They all run in to the warm fire,
Outside it's getting rather dire,
They're happy, jolly and merry!
Christmas is coming,
With angels, stars and a tree,
They're happy, jolly and merry!
Through the window all you can see,
Is the children running around in glee,
They're happy, jolly and merry!
They build a snowman,
As quick as they can,
They're happy, jolly and merry!
At last Christmas has come,
And they're all having fun,
They're happy, jolly and merry!

Jessica Norrie (12)
Insch Primary School, Insch

LOOKING OUT THE WINDOW

I looked out the window
On Christmas morning,
Hoping to see what I had never seen before;
Snow falling like confetti.

I looked up and saw
Icicles hanging from the windows
And spider webs hung like curtains on the grass,
Glistening in the sun.

Behind me there was a
Bone-chilling breath of cold winter air
And even creeping through my
Warm, woolly clothes.

Again I looked outside
And saw two little robins hopping about,
For the last berry,
Hoping that they would not have to starve.

Children make snowmen
And going down steep hills on sledges
And slipping on the cold floor
Of frost and ice.

Abby Kelman (11)
Insch Primary School, Insch

Snowy Sundays

The robin sits upon the church
on one cold Sunday morning.
Watching the twinkling icicles
and frosty grass below.
Whispering snowflakes falling quietly.
Then he stops and swoops down low
to where the scarves are walking.
Woolly hats and woolly gloves made for that morning.
Seeing fires through the windows
gives the robin warmth.
But no one knows how he feels
as the rest of the birds fly north.
The snowman stands beside the pond
where the ice is cracking.
But no one hears the silence and peace
there on that winter's morning.

Nicola Farquhar (11)
Insch Primary School, Insch

Snow On The Ground Is Like Crystals And Diamonds

Snow on the ground is like crystals and diamonds
And for when you see icicles, you hear them twinkling
Twinkling icicles
When you walk on the grass when it's frosty
It crunches under your feet, frosty grass
Snow on the ground is like crystals and diamonds
And when you see robins chirping and digging for worms
You feel sorry for them, chirping robins
When walking on ice you can hear it cracking beneath you
Cracking ice
Snow on the ground is like crystals and diamonds
And when you get home, you sit by the fire
So warm, warm fire
Then when in bed you remember the day so good
And think of the world that is beautiful when it's winter
Snow on the ground is like crystals and diamonds.

Tania Moir (11)
Insch Primary School, Insch

Hallowe'en

Spooky spirits
Are after you,
Giants are scary
And vampires too.

Wicked witches
And dreadful cats,
Scary skeletons
And big black bats.

Ghastly goblins,
Evil dummies,
Deadly Dracula,
Ancient mummies.

They're all scary
And after you,
They'll come up behind
And shout out *boo!*

Calum Howard (11)
Kennethmont School, Huntly

PC Pig

PC Pig was a very fat pig,
He went to a disco and did a jig
He fell right over onto his big fat tum
And rolled straight over onto his big fat bum.

Darryl McLaughlin (11)
Kennethmont School, Huntly

Dumbstruck

I'm stuck for words,
Don't know what to write,
If I don't get a move on,
I'll be here 'til night.

This writing is hard,
I want some fun,
I need some help,
To get this work done.

I want to leave,
I want to go home,
This writing is boring,
I wish I could leave it alone.

Finally, I'm finished,
Done what I had to do,
I'm happy that I'm finished,
This hullabaloo!

Rhuaraidh Docherty (11)
Kennethmont School, Huntly

The Moon

The moon is in the sky
I wish I could see the moon
But I dream about it
I wake but I cannot see it
I might go and tell my friends but
They might not listen.

Fiona Webster (9)
Kennethmont School, Huntly

THE SUN

The sun is a great big ball,
Burning in the sky,
When the sun is out, my friends come to call for me,
Everyone likes the sun, they wave as they pass by,
The sun can make us happy,
The sun can make us cry,
It's always nice to see the sun,
But it can also make us die,
As the sun goes down at night, it sets the sky aglow,
Some people come out to take a photo,
Where it goes at night, no one really knows.

Sean Webb (11)
Kennethmont School, Huntly

AUTUMN

Autumn is the time of year,
Umbrellas begin to appear,
This is the time when we get dark nights,
When you go out, you will need lights.

Leaves are falling from the trees,
Which fills the children full of glee,
For leaves are very fun to jump in,
Leaves the ground-keepers busy rakin'.

Liam Paterson (10)
Kennethmont School, Huntly

A Week As A Toilet

Monday morning, fresh and clean,
A lovely shiny bowl,
That cleaner in the apron
Is a very cheery soul.

Tuesday, someone rushes in,
They're really in a hurry,
The door slams shut and they sit down,
They've just eaten a curry.

Wednesday, my handle's broke,
The paper's piling high,
Please hurry up and fix me,
Or I think I'm going to cry.

Thursday, no one visits me,
Now I'm *out of order*,
I wish they would just fix me,
Doing nothing is just murder.

Friday, my handle's sorted,
I'm in action once again,
They are in and out of here all day,
Sometimes it is a pain.

Saturday, it's busy,
Lots of people in a rush,
One after another,
Just a never-ending flush.

Sunday, it is quiet,
The doors are shut today,
It all starts again tomorrow,
Another working day.

Ryan Dawson (10)
Kennethmont School, Huntly

Lonely

I'm feeling very lonely,
But I'm really not sure why.
I'm just a little toddler,
Staring at the sky.
I'm lost and I can't find my mum,
She's wandered far away.
I hope she comes to find me soon,
I need her here to play.
It's getting scary in the dark,
I want to go back home,
It really gets upsetting,
When you're lost and all alone.

Katy Campbell (10)
Kennethmont School, Huntly

Stars

I think it is called a star
They are way out far
They come out at night
They're really bright
And they're just like a light
They are in the sky
I wonder why?
When they go away
I wonder where they are all day?

Lorna Gordon (9)
Kennethmont School, Huntly

My Puppy, Charlie

Charlie is a puppy
He jumps up and down
He is like a frog
He is funnier than a clown

I love my little pup
I will miss him when he goes
I'll miss the way he knocks my cup
I will miss his little pink nose

I'll miss the way he looks at me
I'll miss the way he barks I will feel very lonely
'Cause he is not here with me now.

Ashley Cruickshank (10)
Kennethmont School, Huntly

Horses

Horses are mammals,
They are quite big,
I have a horse
And he eats like a pig.

My Shetland is cute,
She has small feet,
Horses eat grass,
They don't eat meat.

Kirsten Docherty (10)
Kennethmont School, Huntly

At Night

At night I looked up in the sky,
I saw a spaceship flying by
And watching the stars away up high,
Now I think I want to cry,
The moon is big and bright and light,
I think it's such a beautiful sight,
I think the moon is a cheesy-white
And I think it spies on me every night.

Amy Grant (11)
Kennethmont School, Huntly

Stars

Stars are in the sky
I just wonder why
If other people can see them
So can I
I see them every night
They're like a big light.

Claire Drysdale (9)
Kennethmont School, Huntly

Dolphins

Dolphins are big and blue,
Oh how I love them I do,
I see them swimming around in the sea
And I say to myself, come I wish they would
Come and stay with me.

Emily Phillips (10)
Kennethmont School, Huntly

An Autumn Morning

I see golden leaves like fire in the trees,
I hear cars stalling madly in the car park,
I smell leaves burning like paper,
I taste the fresh air like water in my mouth,
I feel the frost building up in my hands,
I feel sad because autumn is nearly gone.

Andrew Mair (8)
Mintlaw Primary School, Peterhead

An Autumn Morning

I see frost glittering and glinting on the pavement,
I hear the birds singing in the frost-covered trees,
I smell the cold air going up my nose,
I taste the fresh air when I breathe in,
I feel the cold frost in my hands,
I am happy that autumn has come.

Ellen Bain (8)
Mintlaw Primary School, Peterhead

An Autumn Morning

I see a tree nearly bare with leaves golden and brown,
I hear cars clunking and crashing,
I smell the air up my nose,
I taste the sweet fresh air,
I feel the breeze that makes me shiver wildly,
I feel warm and snug with my hat and scarf.

Craig Hutcheon (8)
Mintlaw Primary School, Peterhead

An Autumn Morning

I see glittery feathery frost on the ground,
I hear birds through the frosty wind,
I smell the cold air in my nose,
I taste the dampness as it goes into the air,
I feel the slippery ice with my feet,
I feel happy because autumn has come.

Lisa Sutherland (8)
Mintlaw Primary School, Peterhead

An Autumn Morning

I see people skidding across the glittery ice,
I hear the glistening ice shatter,
I smell the exhaust fumes,
I taste the cold air blowing into my mouth,
I feel the cold air whistling on my back,
I feel warm in my big blue coat.

Dale Nicoll (8)
Mintlaw Primary School, Peterhead

An Autumn Morning

I see golden leaves falling off trees
I hear birds singing from the branches
I smell the last of the summer flowers
I taste cold air going up my nose
I feel the frost nipping my fingers
I feel happy.

Karen Hayward (8)
Mintlaw Primary School, Peterhead

An Autumn Morning

I see the fiery leaves blowing in the wind
And the ice melting in my hand,
I hear the birds singing on the fence post
And people trying to start their cars in anger,
I smell the freezing cold air
And the smoke coming from chimney tops,
I taste the cold, icy air
And I feel the cold wind on my back
Like twigs rubbing against me
But I feel nice and snug in my hat and coat.

Michael Howie (9)
Mintlaw Primary School, Peterhead

An Autumn Morning

I feel the frost on my window
It was gritty
I hear the icy leaves crunching
I smell the car exhaust pipe
I taste the cold on my face
I feel the frost on my hands
I feel happy that autumn has come.

Alistair McKay (8)
Mintlaw Primary School, Peterhead

An Autumn Morning

I see my breath at the window like steam,
I hear the kettle flick,
I smell dampness coming from the open window,
I taste the air from my mouth,
I feel the wind blowing at my face,
I feel happy because it is autumn.

Billie-Jo Monaghan (8)
Mintlaw Primary School, Peterhead

Harry Potter

Swinging your wand
From side to side,
Then sit back and enjoy the ride,
Alakazam, alakazoo,
Hey, it's great,
We're on a choo-choo.
They collect the tickets,
One by one,
This is really so much fun.

Matthew Banks (10)
Port Elphinstone Primary School, Inverurie

The Hurricane

The hurricane sweeps rain across the ground,
It blows rooftops off the houses,
It shatters windows
And is really scary.
It topples cars,
It lifts caravans off the ground,
It makes tidal waves
And blows down trees,
It blows down power lines,
Leaves go flying past
As it screams defiance.

Joshua Michie (9)
Port Elphinstone Primary School, Inverurie

Roller Coasters

Whizzing up and down is fun,
Twirling round in the sun,
Spinning round in the sky,
Way up so very high.
I love it so much,
It's my favourite thing to do
And I think you should do it too.

Kareen Webster (9)
Port Elphinstone Primary School, Inverurie

Mad

When I am mad I have a strop,
I am cheeky to my mum,
She sends me up to my room
And tells me to stop.

I stamp my feet
And throw my toys,
My mum shouts to me,
'If you don't stop that awful noise
You can't play with the boys.'

Callum Murray (9)
Port Elphinstone Primary School, Inverurie

My Cat

I love my cat,
He sleeps so peacefully
On a bright mat.
He brings me this, he brings that,
He's my cat, my cat.
He is the best,
I think he is better than all the rest.

Vikki Mennie (9)
Port Elphinstone Primary School, Inverurie

SWEETS

Sweets are my favourite food,
But I don't get them when I'm in a mood,
I don't have a favourite sweet you see,
Every sweet is right for me.
Chocolate, wine gums, Polos too,
I will not share any with you.
Soft mints, chewits and pastilles too,
Lots of things for me and you.
So don't you touch my sweets you see
Cos they're all for me! *Me! Me!*

Laura Mackie (9)
Port Elphinstone Primary School, Inverurie

SWEETS

There are green sweets,
There are yellow sweets,
There are blue sweets,
There are purple sweets,
But I just can't choose!
They are all so yummy,
To fill my tummy,
I'll have to choose them all.

David Ferguson (9)
Port Elphinstone Primary School, Inverurie

Jump Jet

J is for jumping in the park
U is for turning a U-turn in a car
M is for money in the city bank
P is for the jet plane

J is for the jump jet
E is for flight experience
T is for travelling with an airline.

Frazer Christie (10)
Port Elphinstone Primary School, Inverurie

My Naughty Dog

My dog is very naughty,
He chews all our shoes,
He chases our cat
And gets us in a flap.
He pulls and pulls his lead,
Until we let him go,
Then he runs and runs and runs,
Until he's out of breath.

Lisa Finnigan (9)
Port Elphinstone Primary School, Inverurie

The Witch

A witch,
Her eyes great green,
Nose pointed,
Giant nostrils,
Her mouth wrinkled,
Teeth rotten with black holes,
Voice cackly as a frog's laugh,
Beefy horrible breath,
Skin wrinkly as an old woman's,
Her hair as black as can be,
Her nails as sharp as her hat,
With filthy dirty black shoes,
Because of her dragging them across the graveyard,
Her familiars - a cat and a bat.

Liam Noble (8)
St Andrew's Primary School, Fraserburgh

The Witch

A ghastly witch with eyes like ice,
Had a long hooked nose,
Like a nail,
Which she used to stab children,
One black tooth in her mouth,
A wart on each hand
And a threadbare cloak,
In her deserted cottage,
Feeding her familiar,
A vampire bat.

Sarah-Marie Gault (8)
St Andrew's Primary School, Fraserburgh

The Witch With Violet Eyes

A crooked witch,
With violet eyes,
Flew out one scary night,
A nose with a wart
And her teeth all cracked,
Her skin all bumpy
And her voice was scary,
Her hair was tangled,
Her breath was smelly and horrible,
Her nails were as sharp as a knife,
They were so dirty,
Her clothes were as black as the starry sky,
Her boots were sharp
And she had a familiar cat,
Black with fangs hanging down,
As she stirred her cauldron.

Kirsty Alexander (8)
St Andrew's Primary School, Fraserburgh

The Evil Witch

Once an evil witch,
With a terrible voice,
Roamed the dark scary woods,
Her cloak was mud-stained,
She had a terrible black cat,
She roams the night skies
On her broomstick
And she hates all humanity.

Joshua Masson (8)
St Andrew's Primary School, Fraserburgh

The Witch

A witch I know has luminous eyes
And a face as green as a lime,
Her nose has a wart,
With warts on her wart,
A lipless mouth,
But teeth sharp as sharp as carving knives,
Her voice is as loud as a wild wolf's howl,
Lice crawl in her hair,
Nails as long as daggers
And with every breath she takes,
A person dies,
As her crafty cat glows luminous,
In the darkness of the night.

Stephen Watt (8)
St Andrew's Primary School, Fraserburgh

Witch

A hideous witch,
Lived in a horrible ditch,
With white eyes and a crooked nose,
A lumpy mouth and a magic black tooth.

Leathery skin has she,
Tangled hair and filthy nails,
Her boots go *clip-clop*
With her wicked black cat
Following behind.

Hayley McIntosh (8)
St Andrew's Primary School, Fraserburgh

LAND OF ICE

The land is icy,
Icy cold,
The wind,
Perishing and bold,
So cold,
But the sun,
Glinting in the sky,
The ice sparkling,
Shiny bright,
The sea still,
No waves at all,
The wind has gone,
So it's silent,
No sound at all,
The land is wonderful,
The ice is glistening,
The sun out high in the big bright sky.

Alistair Eddie (9)
St Andrew's Primary School, Fraserburgh

THE WITCH

There is a witch,
Her face pale and hideous,
Beady eyes staring at me,
Her nose just two slits,
Her mouth is a scowl,
She has one tooth,
Her nails as sharp as knives,
Her familiar, a dragon guards her,
As she mixes her slimy potions.

Calum MacLeod (8)
St Andrew's Primary School, Fraserburgh

The Witch

An old witch,
Rocking in her rocking chair,
With hideous skin,
Beady little eyes,
As yellow as sunlight,
A nose like a troll's,
A tight-lipped mouth,
Her hair black and curled,
Her nails as sharp as a parrot's claw,
Her voice is cracked but still evil,
She has an owl so hairy
And can I mention,
That the owl is a lot like her!

Steven Buchan (8)
St Andrew's Primary School, Fraserburgh

Land Of Ice

The land of ice so perishing and bitter,
The snow blizzard coming down,
The howling of wolves,
The ice sparkling shiny like jewels,
The noise of whales slashing about,
The sea crunching the ice,
The wind stormy, whistling about,
It was icy and misty,
In the land of ice.

Emma May (8)
St Andrew's Primary School, Fraserburgh

The Witch

A witch! A witch!
Eyes made of blood,
Mouth like a mouse, as quiet as a mouse,
Teeth made of rotten potions,
Skin so hard like rubber and grease,
Long hair covering her face,
Hideous long smelly nails,
Pointed shoes,
Long hooded cloak, purple and red,
Her pet bat with long black teeth,
Lives with her under the pier,
Beware!
You're in for a scare!

Christopher Mackie (8)
St Andrew's Primary School, Fraserburgh

The Land Of The Midnight Sun

It is sunny now in the Arctic,
In the land of the midnight sun,
The shimmering jewel-like crystals
Are sparkling for everyone,
The sea is calm,
There is no sound,
There is no wind in the air,
So beautiful,
The land of the midnight sun.

Sarah-Jane Bisset (8)
St Andrew's Primary School, Fraserburgh

The Witch

A hideous witch lived in a graveyard,
With her black cat that likes the darkness,
Her burning eyes glow in the dark
And her nose is covered in warts,
Her mouth is purple and her teeth are split in half,
Her skin is dark and her hair is black,
Her nails are long and split,
Her hat is high peaked
And she holds a broomstick that she rides at night,
Her cauldron holds human flesh,
People's heads and hearts,
With a disgusting stench.

Ross West (8)
St Andrew's Primary School, Fraserburgh

The Witch

There is a hideous witch,
Who lives in the forest,
In a burnt-out tree,
She has dark red eyes
That glow,
She wears a filthy black cloak
And has a bent nose,
She has a broomstick
And a snake,
She has a long black hat.

Neil Holland (8)
St Andrew's Primary School, Fraserburgh

IBROX PARK

Ibrox Park is where Rangers play
I am going to see them today
At six o'clock we arrive there
And a drunkie gives me a scare
We go into the stadium and take our seats
We've got our grub, good let's eat
The ref blows his whistle and starts
The match against Cally Thistle
Five minutes later Rangers score
The crowd they scream and roar
Rangers are proud of their first goal
A great one scored by Flo
People are thumping the seats and under my feet
I feel the beats.

Austin Lennon (11)
St Gerardine Primary School, Lossiemouth

ZOOGO'S MISTAKE

Zap zap Zoogo's zaps,
He zaps, he shoots,
He hits, he swoops,
Hitting bottles, missing models,
As he tries to beat his record,
He accidentally zapped his cupboard,
When it falls miles and miles,
He tries to get it but he doesn't,
As it falls down to Earth as a wee boy,
Tries to fit the clothes on,
The cupboard ends up in the bin,
So that is Zoogo's cupboard
And he never wants to hit again.

Craig Smith (10)
St Gerardine Primary School, Lossiemouth

WINTER

Winter is fun
Winter is cold
You can't run
It's time to make sculptures without a mould,
At Christmas Eve you go to bed
And wait for Santa to come at night,
To come at night,
So we scrunch into a tight ball,
Holding a round white teddy bear,
When it's Christmas Day we're all amazed
And we stand and gaze,
We play and play,
We can't go out, we want to stay,
So your mum and dad sigh
And keep one eagle eye and sigh.

Sean McEneany (9)
St Gerardine Primary School, Lossiemouth

THE FRIENDLY HORSE

Jump on a horse, off we go
Trotting through fields, row after row
Bouncing up and down as we jump
Over the bars that go bump
Time to start going faster
Like a tube of flying pasta
I'm getting tired now
Time to slow down
I'll put you in your stable now
It's time for you to have a rest
Until tomorrow when we start again.

Ruth Corps (10)
St Gerardine Primary School, Lossiemouth

Excuse Me Mr Robin

'Excuse me Mr Robin
How are you today?
I have a little favour
To ask of you my friend.'
'What is that?' replied the robin.
'Would you mind to help
Because I'm lost and fearful
In this scary little place?'
'Oh dear,' sighed Mr Robin
(I only just heard what he said.)
'I would like it if you could
Please lead me out of this horrible, creepy wood.'
'Of course I'll help,' replied the robin,
'That is why I'm here.'
'Why thank you Mr Robin,
Thank you for your help.'
'You're welcome little pussy cat
Do not get lost again.'

Charlotte Fairminer (11)
St Gerardine Primary School, Lossiemouth

Fish On The Plate

I am a fish,
I am stuck here on this plate,
I used to wiggle and wriggle in the river,
But now I am stuck on this plate with mash and peas,
The river used to splash and splish and splosh,
But now I'll never know 'cause I'm stuck on this plate beside you,
I used to play with all my friends,
But now I am stuck here on this plate . . . it's too late!

Claire Matthews (11)
St Gerardine Primary School, Lossiemouth

FREE WORLD

The bird is free
He soars and swoops
He can reach the highest of high
And the lowest of low

The bird is free
He touches the sky
And skims the waters

The bird is free
No destination
No reason to stay
No place to reach

The bird is free
He has not a care in the world
He is able to be free
In this harsh and unpleasant land.

Emily Alldritt (10)
St Gerardine Primary School, Lossiemouth

DAVID BECKHAM

David Beckham for Man U
He takes the kicks to show
Me and you
He plays midfield, number seven
Scores a hat-trick in football heaven

On his way in his BM
To old Trafford to win again
If they win, they're in the final
David Beckham is my idol!

Ewan Thomson (11)
St Gerardine Primary School, Lossiemouth

10 LITTLE BLACKBIRDS

10 little blackbirds sitting in a line,
One flew off and then there were 9.

9 little blackbirds sitting on a gate,
One had a meeting so then there were 8.

8 little blackbirds sitting in Heaven,
One had to go and then there were 7.

7 little blackbirds collecting sticks,
One fell over and then there were 6.

6 little blackbirds sitting on a hive,
One had to get food then there were 5.

5 little blackbirds hopping on the floor,
One tripped over so then there was 4.

4 little blackbirds sitting in a tree,
A baby was calling so then there were 3.

3 little blackbirds one with the flu,
It went home so then there were 2.

2 little blackbirds, one bought a bun,
The other one was jealous so then there was 1.

1 little blackbird sitting all alone,
'I am so lonely, I think I'll go home.'

Chloe McKay (10)
St Gerardine Primary School, Lossiemouth

BROTHERS ARE ANNOYING

Brothers are a pain,
Andrew moans and groans.
Taller David shouts at me!
Every time when I come home
The two wicked brothers await.

Andrew always trips me up,
David always laughs.
They always throw stuff at me
And call me wicked names.

Why don't they leave me alone?
They're always on my case.
Chasing me and bullying me,
Not letting me watch television,
Wicked brothers please go away!

Hannah Gordon (11)
St Gerardine Primary School, Lossiemouth

MY GRANNY

My granny is a pearl of wisdom waiting to be found,
She helped me with a poem when no one was around.
We walk together all the time when the sun is fine and bright,
She looks after me when I'm ill and makes sure I'm alright.
My gran, she makes the best chips in the whole of Lossie town,
I'm sure she still does cancan dancing when wearing her nightgown.
My gran watches Bargain Hunt, she hopes she'll find she has an antique,
I'm glad my gran is my gran, she simply is unique!

Sean Cross (11)
St Gerardine Primary School, Lossiemouth

D-Day

As they left their cruisers
To dock on the bay
To fight for freedom
Guns fired from each side
Planes swooshing over land and the sea
Bang! The wires are broken and the soldiers run on through
Across the minefield
Towards victory
When they get to Heaven
To St Peter, they will tell
More soldiers reporting, Sir
Didn't we do well?

Michael McLeod (10)
St Gerardine Primary School, Lossiemouth

Lord Of The Rings, The Two Towers

Nqzgûl soaring through the sky
Ringwraith's hoping Frodo will die
Hobbits running to and fro
To Mordor the Fellowship must go

Uruk-hai elves and men fight it out
In an electrifying, magnificent bout
Ents are big trees that walk
Trees that even talk.

Ross Diack (11)
St Gerardine Primary School, Lossiemouth

The Future

A hundred years from now,
In twenty-one hundred and three,
A massive ice age engulfs the Earth,
No animals to see.

In twenty-nine hundred and two,
The Earth is even worse,
A massive meteor strikes the ground,
It has to be a curse.

In thirty-one hundred and two,
Some life is remaining,
But if you want to see it,
Well, that's a lot of waiting!

Christopher Jennings (11)
St Gerardine Primary School, Lossiemouth

Top Dog

Down in the junkyard,
Buster roams,
Breaking bottles, kicking cones.

Clambering up the garbage heap,
Leaping, lapping dogs he meets.

To them he is the king of all,
Always playing with his ball!

Charlotte Wilson (10)
St Gerardine Primary School, Lossiemouth

HENRIK LARSSON

H is for the headers that Larsson always scores.
E is for excellence in inventing new tricks.
N is for narrow headers that he always scores.
R is for the raging crowds when Henrik scores.
I is for intelligence that he always uses.
K is for the kicks that never miss the target.

L is for the looks according to the women!
A is for accurate passing.
R is for running quickly down the line.
S is for swerve when the ball curls in.
S is for the seven he wears with pride.
O is for O'Neil, his best manager ever.
N is for never losing his determination.

Gary Campbell (11)
St Gerardine Primary School, Lossiemouth

AT THE BEACH

The birds *quack*
The waves *splash*
On the glistening sand

As the water splashes against the seaweed
The dark, gooey, browny and greeny seaweed
Covers the rocks

As water splashes against the boat
A wave drives fish faster
The seaweed sticks to the side of the boat.

Malcolm Hendry (10)
St Gerardine Primary School, Lossiemouth

At The Horses' Stable

At the horses' stable,
The horses began to neigh,
I went up and patted their silk, black coats,
All of them stopped, except one named Oliver!
That one named Oliver,
Galloped around in the soft, squidgy mud,
Rolled over the place until his silky, black coat
Was covered in brown mud!

I love the horses at Covesea,
They're fun,
They're cheeky,
They're the best!

Kirsty Smith (10)
St Gerardine Primary School, Lossiemouth

Puppies

Puppies like to chew and play
The day away,
They play with toys all over the floor,
Up the stairs and out of the door.
They run about, chasing their tails,
So fast, they're certainly not slow like snails.
When all that playing tires them out,
They find it very hard to shout.
When it is time for their beds,
You say goodnight and kiss their heads.

Kirsteen Richardson (11)
St Gerardine Primary School, Lossiemouth

Shadow

Shadow is as black as coal,
He has a chest as white as a cloud.
Shadow is as cute as a baby,
But he is not very bright at all.
He chases his tail
And crashes into the door,
Before falling on the floor.
He's my little Shadow.

Shadow likes chasing birds,
He loves getting cuddles.
He likes going on long walks,
Unless there are cats about.
Shadow is thin and small,
He's one year old
And he loves his dinner.
I think he's a winner,
He's my little Shadow.

Rhuraidh Garness (11)
St Gerardine Primary School, Lossiemouth

Summer

S is for school holidays.
U is for umbrellas in the sand.
M is for mountainous sand dunes.
M is for making sandcastles.
E is for everlasting sunshine.
R is for running to the beach.

Daniel Baker (11)
St Gerardine Primary School, Lossiemouth

I Wish I Were A Rabbit

I wish I were a rabbit
All furry and black,
With long floppy ears,
That lay across my back.
The whole of me is neat,
Including my feet.
My tail is bushy like a rose,
All the time I wiggle my nose.
I have a run where I can play
And at night I sleep on a bed of hay.

Zara Petrie (11)
St Gerardine Primary School, Lossiemouth

A Friend

A friend who is there,
Will always care.
A friend is funny,
Full of laughter.
A friend is someone who makes you smile,
Right from the start to the very end.
A friend is someone who is honest,
Never telling lies.
A friend is great to have around,
So stick with them and don't be sad.

Emily Stewart (10)
St Gerardine Primary School, Lossiemouth

Chameleon's Revenge

In the sun the chameleon lay
Waiting for a tasty prey
Then buzzing by comes Mr Fly
And as quick as a flash he's turned into *pie!*
Suddenly a spider comes
And starts to eat all the flies
The chameleon gets mad, *look!*
The spider's a *snack!*
The chameleon smiles and said to himself
That was nice, let's try it again!
Ha, ha, ha!

Alexander Florence (11)
St Gerardine Primary School, Lossiemouth

War

Crashing on shore,
Bullets getting fired
At me and my army.
Sand in my boots,
Barbed wire pricking in,
Bombs exploding all around.
Empty shells left lying on the ground.
Death after death,
My army disappears.
My friend and I survive,
To the end.

Frazer McKechnie (11)
St Gerardine Primary School, Lossiemouth

SPIDER MAD

Spider fangs go *cling, clang*
As they stalk their prey
Then they attack and . . .
Down goes Mr Fly
Now I'll chuck him in the web
He won't get out, he's way dead
Now I'll go and get some more
For my winter supplies
Actually I'm not that bad
I'm even worse
Ha, ha, ha!

Culum Graham (10)
St Gerardine Primary School, Lossiemouth

SNOW

Snow is as white as a football being kicked
Around in a field,
Snow is stars flashing speedily
Around in the sky,
Snow is glistening ice cubes
Getting dropped into a glass,
Snow is a fluffy cloud
Floating high above the sky.

Michael Spring (11)
St Gerardine Primary School, Lossiemouth

SPACESHIP

S is for the stars shining bright.
P is for planets circling the sun.
A is for astronauts getting information.
C is for the comets speeding till they hit something.
E is for the eclipse, a minute of darkness.
S is for the solar system holding all the planets.
H is for the hydrogen hiding in the stars.
I is for the inner core burning inside the sun.
P is for the probes sent to other planets.

William Clunas (11)
St Gerardine Primary School, Lossiemouth

LEAVES

Leaves, leaves falling to the ground,
Caught my eye one day,
Falling from the sky,
Landed on a man's tie.

It fell miles and miles
And fell onto hard concrete,
On the city's floor.

Laurie Gill (10)
St Gerardine Primary School, Lossiemouth

School

S chool is maths,
C alculating algebraic equations,
H alves, percentages and decimals,
O btuse angles, reflex or acute,
O rdering numbers, negative or positive?
L anguage so complicated, what is tessellation?

Amy McLeod (11)
St Gerardine Primary School, Lossiemouth

School

School, what can I say about school?
School can be fun sometimes,
School can be boring sometimes,
School is fun when we go to the gym,
School is boring when we go to maths,
But the best bit of all is going home.

Chelsea Logan (10)
St Gerardine Primary School, Lossiemouth

Jaws

Jaws is raging under the world in the deep ocean,
The rusty moon blazing down,
The speeding wind leaks out a cry,
Chewing through the fishermen's net,
Hunting down his prey,
Always where the fishermen don't want him to be.

Joseph Fleetwood (11)
St Gerardine Primary School, Lossiemouth

The Silver Horse

She plays with the eagle
She races the wind
Even though she always wins
The silver horse never lies
The silver horse will never die
She's warm like the sun
She shines like the moon
She will dance with the stars until the early noon.

Chelsea Cruickshank (11)
St Gerardine Primary School, Lossiemouth

Snowbody Loves Me

Snowbody loves me, I am living in a hole
Snowbody loves me, I am a little soul
I lost my mum and dad
If I don't see them today, I think I will go mad
Snowbody loves me, though I was so comfy
On my *mother's* coat
The heat was heart-warming
But now I am alone
Snowbody loves me
I just can't see why
People love others
But snowbody loves me.

Jordan Stuart (10)
St Sylvester's Primary School, Elgin

I Wish

S is for space
P is for Pluto
A is for asteroids
   wish I were an astronaut
C is for Challenger
E is for Earth

A is for aliens
L is for lunar
I is for intergalactic
E is for eclipse
   wish I remembered shades
N is for nebula
S is for the solar system
   wish my life away.

Anthony Brannigan (9)
St Sylvester's Primary School, Elgin

Watch What You Call Me!

Twinkle twinkle chocolate bar
What you say is what you are
If you say it back to me
You're a hairy . . .
Chimpanzee!

Louise Masson (10)
St Sylvester's Primary School, Elgin

All About Snowy

My name is Snowy,
I'm 3 months old,
I live in the Arctic,
A place that is icy cold.

I sleep in a hole
And dream of being cosy,
Somewhere sunny and warm,
That'll keep me toastie!

Until that time
I'll have to make do
And cuddle up close to
My mummy!

Stephanie Parry (10)
St Sylvester's Primary School, Elgin

My Brother

My brother is a pain
He drives me insane
My mum says, 'Don't do that.'
But Trevor said, 'I hate you!'
And ran off
But I still love him
That's my brother.

Jodie Jones (10)
St Sylvester's Primary School, Elgin

Fuzz

Hello everyone, my name is Fuzz
All the bees chase me with a buzz
Others say I'm a handsome bear
And so they should, I'm really quite rare
Big, mean bullies bully me
So I just call a stinger bee

When I'm in trouble
Stinger bees on the double
I just call, 'Stinger bee!'
Then he just comes to me
'Come and help me stinger bee
I need you to rescue me.'

Melissa Grant (10)
St Sylvester's Primary School, Elgin

Dad

All around me I can see clouds; you and me,
It's so good, just you and me,
I can't believe I am with you now,
I don't just want to stand and wait,
I want to hug you,
You silly dad,
I don't want to go,
But it's just too late.

Katrina Andrews (9)
St Sylvester's Primary School, Elgin

Sammy!

Sammy was a little ball
A little ball of fur
Now each day he gets bigger
And bigger
And this is what we say,
Sammy runs,
Sammy turns,
What's his name?
Sammy Burns!

Heather Burns (11)
St Sylvester's Primary School, Elgin

Songs Of The Sea

The dolphins dive up into the sky,
Like baby birds trying to fly,
Splashing about in the calm blue sea,
Singing their songs with so much glee,
In my mind I can see them leap,
I wish I could join them in the deep!

Amber Hayward (10)
St Sylvester's Primary School, Elgin

Our Name Is Boo

My mum calls me Boo
And I call her that too
We will always be together
One and two,
forever!

Agnes Neal (10)
St Sylvester's Primary School, Elgin

The Solar System

The Milky Way's a sweetie,
Pluto is a golf ball
The rings of Saturn are doughnuts,
Jupiter's a giant,
The moon is made of cheese,
The Earth's a glass of water,
The sun's a red hot chilli,
Mercury's a hot potato and
Venus is an orange just according
To *me!*

Barry James Moir (10)
St Sylvester's Primary School, Elgin

Dolphins

Dolphins are mammals
They swim in the sea
Friendly and graceful
A pleasure to see

They swim very fast
Through the rough and calm sea
Playful and cheeky
Like my sister and me.

Kerry Hesten (10)
St Sylvester's Primary School, Elgin

What Can I Say?

What can I say?
What can I do?
What can I love?
What can I learn?
Is there a soul out there for me
In this lonely desert of space?
A desert of space with planets,
No sign of life,
No sign of life.

Will I get back to Earth?
Will I live to see the day of my first child being born?
See my wife smiling,
Holding my newborn baby girl or boy?
See them growing up?
My child getting married?

Claire Morrison (11)
St Thomas' RC Primary School, Keith

Space

Space is cool, it rules
We can see space dust in space
A meteorite is coming, we must hide
They don't know it's coming to Earth
The meteorite has blown up in space.

Gary Mitchell (11)
St Thomas' RC Primary School, Keith

Blast-Off

I would miss . . .

Being paid for working on the farm
Playing with my friends in the playground
The terrible, terrorising Caitlin
Eilidh's constant crying
Mum's moaning
Dad's nagging about going to bed
Playing endlessly with my PS2
Playing in my room and sleeping
Going dooking in the summer
Climbing trees in the garden

Blast-off!

Craig Sims (10)
St Thomas' RC Primary School, Keith

Stars

When the stars come out at night
My brother always gets a fright
I always look at the lovely sight
They're always at such a high height
But believe me
They are *so* bright!

Laura Bowie (9)
St Thomas' RC Primary School, Keith

Blast-Off!

I would miss my comfy bed
I would miss my loud stereo
I would miss my rabbit's destructive habits
I would miss my cool 'Spyro the Dragon' game
I would miss my mum and dad who cheer me up when I'm
in a bad mood
I would miss my fast bike
I would miss the friendliness of our school
I would miss the fellowship of St Peter's Church
I would miss my classmates
I would miss my friends

Blast-off!

Robert Main (11)
St Thomas' RC Primary School, Keith

Sun And Moon

I am head of all stars and the universe
I will not let these planets push me around
All these long days, I just watch the planets pass by
There's worlds out there waiting to be found
But will I ever see them?

The man on the moon
I only come at night when the stars shine bright
The love of my life is the beautiful sun
What shall I say to that woman staring at me?

Rachel McKay (11)
St Thomas' RC Primary School, Keith

BLAST OFF

I would miss the best dad in the world because he is *my* dad
I would miss my mum because I love her
I would definitely miss my dog because she eats everything
I would miss my friends
I would miss my brother's pestering and play-fights
I would miss my cousins mucking about in my house because
it is quite funny
I would miss Mr Farrell's constant moaning
I would miss my teacher, Ms Francis because she is the best
teacher in the world
I would miss my snugly warm bed
I would miss my planet Earth.

Sophie Webster (11)
St Thomas' RC Primary School, Keith

COUNTDOWN

The smell of newly laid tar
I'd miss my sister when she has one of her mood swings
I would miss my job and my teammates
I'd miss the sparkling of the metallic floor
I would especially miss the smell of the leather seats in my Subaru
I'd really miss my dogs, Rex and Sid
I would miss my friends and our nights out
I'd miss my parents' constant moaning
I would miss my Ferrari V50 and Subaru
I would really miss my girlfriend very much.

Gary Smith (11)
St Thomas' RC Primary School, Keith

Stars

Stars are shiny
Stars are bright
Stars are only out at night
Stars look lovely in the skies
Stars all twinkle in my eyes.

Jaqui Stewart (9)
St Thomas' RC Primary School, Keith

Seasons

Spring is a happy time,
Sunshine peeping through the clouds,
A good time for playing,
Summer's coming, it's nice and warm,
The breeze is cool and gentle,
Filled with air blowing on your face,
Black and yellow bees in the sky,
Autumn is here now,
A cold time, a windy time, rainy too,
Winter is coming - snow say the children,
Snowmen on the ground,
Carrots for the nose,
Stones for the buttons
And a scarf and hat.

Kyle Lear (8)
Seafield Primary School, Elgin

School

Ring, ring, ring
The bell goes for school
The children all walk in
Their faces a mile long
School again, oh no, not school
We get a spelling test
And mental maths too
RE, language and *maths!*
Maths is my worst subject
When the bell goes again for the end of school
The children run out of school
Secretly the teachers couldn't be happier
They jump on the tables and do you know why?
It's the weekend!

Diane Mackay (10)
Seafield Primary School, Elgin

Stop Racism

Come on people, give racism the red card
Come on people, respect, it's not hard
Come on people, stop calling names
Come on people, black or white, we're just the same
Come on people, these words are not a game
Come on people, don't these words fill you with shame?
Come on people, let's play together
Come on people, let's stop racism all together.

Jenna McKidd & Kelly Noble (10)
Seafield Primary School, Elgin

The Night Of The Drunks

The sound of the drunks raiding the park
Falling and shouting out, crossing the road
The dancers bursting out of the nightclubs
Sweating buckets

The sound of drunks getting into fights
Rusty swings going backwards and forwards
Subway trains passing under the park
A drunk falls into the pond with a big splash
The night of the drunks

The sound of drunks raiding the bins
Smashing car windows, alarms going off
The sound of sirens, smashed bottles
And people shouting from their windows
The night of the drunks.

Callum Ord (11)
Seafield Primary School, Elgin

My Cat

My cat is very silly
The funniest thing she does is run about then she flops over
She climbs up the Christmas tree at Christmas time
We just think she is very funny
She jumps on the older cat
We love them so much.

Katie McKerrell & Sally Lapington (9)
Seafield Primary School, Elgin

TOAST TO THE LASSES

Their bonnie eyes and their sparkly hair
Their nice politeness and loving care
We like the way you sort things out
We like the way you walk about
We like the way you're organised
We like your make-up, it smells so nice
We're not so sure of your lack of fun
But you're definitely funnier than our mums
Your great big smiles are so, so cute
But you really do order us about
Even though you make us mad
You are not really that bad.

Kyle Stewart & Shaun Grant (11)
Seafield Primary School, Elgin

SHOW RACISM DA RED CARD

People black, people white
It doesn't matter, we're both alright

We're all the same
If we weren't, it would be a shame

People hit, people threaten
But I don't care what they reckon

I think people should be friends
For evermore till the world ends.

Jonathan Roe & Cameron Robertson (10)
Seafield Primary School, Elgin

Racism

Racism is evil
Racism is stupid
If racism doesn't stop
I think I'll go mad

Racism is torture
Racism is downright sad
If racism is affecting you
Don't go mad

Show racism the red card
Please, please show racism the red car
Give racism the red card
Please give racism the red card.

Lynsey Blair (10)
Seafield Primary School, Elgin

Dolphin

My dolphin is cute
Cuddly, funny
Playful and smiley
Blue and soft
Gentle and friendly
She makes me happy
I will swim with her.

Alice Stewart (8)
Seafield Primary School, Elgin

Racism

Show racism the red card,
Be nice to people it isn't hard.

People shouting, calling names,
Can't you just join in the games?

Stop racism, it isn't fine,
Can't you just be a friend of mine?

Black and white are just the same,
Come on and join in our game.

Please can you be my friend
And make racism come to an end.

Hayleigh Stephenson (10)
Seafield Primary School, Elgin

The Chase

Cheetah is powerful
Fast
Then the chase
Pounce
The prey is dead
The cheetah has won
Again.

Sean MacDonald (8)
Seafield Primary School, Elgin

Sounds Of The Play Park

Laughing, chattering, gossiping
From the parents
As their toddlers
Whoosh, yelling from the swing
Dogs baring, howling, splashing in the puddles

Little girls slurping on ice cream
Babbling, crying, moaning from the babies
Boys ringing, zooming on their bikes

Teenagers whizzing, rattling, talking on skateboards
Whooping, roaring, screaming
From the roundabout
Then there was silence
They had left.

Kelly Grieve (11)
Seafield Primary School, Elgin

My Teddy

My teddy is soft and cuddly
Cosy to take to bed
And comforting
He is fun to play with
I love to take him to the park.

Ebony Grant (7)
Seafield Primary School, Elgin

Racism

Racism is bad
Racism is cruel
Racism is evil
And stupid too
Racism is dull
Racism is daft
Racism is bonkers
And crazy too
People think it's just a joke
And cool to speak racism
But it's not
Because we all live together on planet Earth.

Brian Walker (10)
Seafield Primary School, Elgin

Dad's Dragon

My dad drew a dragon
He is green
With spikes on his back
He looks hungry
He is blowing fire
From his mouth
He is powerful and big
With sharp teeth and claws
A fierce scary dragon.

Alannah Russell (7)
Seafield Primary School, Elgin

The Twister Is Mad

The twister is mad
He's not very sad
He breaks all the houses
Everyone is sad

The twister is mad
He is very glad
He's worse than my dad
Everyone is sad

The twister is mad
He crashes all the houses
He bashes all the trees
Everyone is sad.

Danny Stuart (11)
Seafield Primary School, Elgin

Dragons

Gigantic dragons starving, bloodthirsty,
Hunting each other,
In front of a castle,
A brave boy wanted to stop them,
He couldn't bear the sight,
But the knights said 'No!'
You might have been the dragon's dessert,
Best to leave them alone.

Sam Watts (8)
Seafield Primary School, Elgin

Show Racism The Red Card

Racism is evil
People that are racist are cowards
Nothing but sad
I think I'd go mad
Racism is torture
Racism is downright sad
If it is affecting you
Don't go mad

Show racism the red card
Please show racism the red card
Show racism the red card
Please, please show racism the red card.

Becky Lapington (10)
Seafield Primary School, Elgin

The Sad Dragon

Once there was a dragon
Beautiful and sad
With sharp teeth and claws
And gigantic wings
She was friendly and kind
But had no friends
She looked too scary
Everyone ran for their lives
Poor dragon.

Connor Kelman (7)
Seafield Primary School, Elgin

FIRE

Help, help, fire, fire,
There's a fire and I can't get out,
I've tried and tried - I've tried so hard
But no one can hear me shout.

I'm scared, I'm frightened, I'm terrified,
The fire will make me sore,
But what's that I hear in the distance?
It's the fire engine's siren roar.

At last they've come to rescue me,
I'm safe and free at last,
I'm really glad this nightmare
Is well and truly passed.

Jorden Davies (10)
Seafield Primary School, Elgin

CHEETAH

Cheetahs are fast
They have sharp teeth
Powerful claws
Spotted camouflage
A predator
Good at hunting
Dangerous and bloodthirsty.

Connor Sutherland (8)
Seafield Primary School, Elgin

The Sunken Wreck

The ship that sunk all those years ago,
Is still down there, way, way below,
The fish swim cautiously all around the wreck,
All the crew are dead and wasting away,
This is all happening way beneath the sea.

These bodies are still there, just in different form,
New coral has been formed,
By the bodies of the dead,
The skulls come alive,
Gems and pearls are their eyes.

All the pearls are shiny and round
And are staring down at the slimy seaweed ground,
The fish have gnawed through the wood on the ship
And found the treasure scattered around,
This is all happening way beneath the sea.

Melissa McKerrell (11)
Seafield Primary School, Elgin

Rhinoceros

Rhinos are strong
Rhinos are smelly
They roll in the mud
They have a fat belly.

Euan Slater (7)
Seafield Primary School, Elgin

To My Friends

My friends are always here for me,
I always have them round for tea,
When we get in trouble,
We never blame each other,
My friends are always here for me.

My friends are always here for me,
I always have them round for tea,
My wee brother always says, 'Can I watch TV?'
He annoys me,
I say, 'Yes,' – he makes a mess.
We always need to tidy up,
My friends always get fed up,
My friends are always there for me!

Natalie Stephen (11)
Seafield Primary School, Elgin

Polar Bear

My polar bear is big and white
It lopes along the snow
It hunts for seals under the ice
Loves to snooze snug hidden away
Lies on the ice to cool down
A great hunter
With powerful teeth and claws.

Rhiannon McAllister (8)
Seafield Primary School, Elgin

Teachers

Teachers getting in their pyjamas,
I'm sure they'd rather go to the Bahamas,
Sunshine, glory, beaches as well,
Oh that would be really swell!
Teaching must be awfully boring,
I'm sure they'd rather be tucked up snoring.

Getting up at 7 o'clock,
It's really boring hearing them talk,
But when it gets to 3.15,
I always hear them shout and scream,
'Hip hip hooray! Hip hip hooray!
I've finished teaching for another day!'

Caasi McCrindle (11)
Seafield Primary School, Elgin

Shep

My dog is amazing
He does all sorts of tricks
To make me laugh
I cuddle my dog no matter what happens
My dog is hairy
Always smiling
Floppy ears flapping
All over the place
He is my best friend.

Kayleigh Ritchie (8)
Seafield Primary School, Elgin

Footie For Life

Football is the life for boys,
Who says us girls can't play,
We like footie just as much as you
And we could play all day.

We'll get on the pitch and show you boys,
That us girls can kick,
You try to show off by running around,
Really, it makes us sick.

Anyone can kick a ball,
Even a dog or cat,
Girls can do the same as boys,
But you boys just don't know that.

Girls can play it as well as boys,
Scoring goals as well,
We can kick a ball about,
Without footie our life would be hell!

Leanne Prescott (11)
Seafield Primary School, Elgin

Spot

My rabbit spot is cuddly
Friendly and fun to play with
He has soft fur
He is gentle and cute
And cosy to cuddle.

Brittany Hulley (7)
Seafield Primary School, Elgin

The Motorcyclist

Fast down the motorway, the motorcyclist goes,
As the grass sways when the wind blows,
Swerving in and out of cars,
Stopping off at all the bars,
He drinks and drives and doesn't care,
The wind still whistling through his hair,
There was a lorry in his sight
And he got such a big fright!

He swerved left and right and hit a tree
And his body and spirit went flying free,
He thought he was in Heaven and thought things well
And then he noticed he was in Hell,
He wished he was nicer and helped people out
And now the Devil makes him shout,
'Help! Let me out!'

Paul McMillan (10)
Seafield Primary School, Elgin

Deserts

D ry and dusty, it is hot
E ndless heat can burn a lot
S inking sand
E verywhere
R ain never comes, so what do I wear?
T oday it is hot and dusty, still
S un is coming, yes it will!

Kristina Nightingale (10)
Seafield Primary School, Elgin

RANGERS

Rangers football team,
They are really mean!
Top of the league,
Never shows fatigue!

Rangers rule
And you are cool,
You play so well,
I think you're swell!

Rangers are the best!
Better than the rest!
I support Rangers,
They are the best!

Johnathon Beveridge (11)
Seafield Primary School, Elgin

TEMPERATE

T oday it's really, really cold,
E very day I have been told,
M other is very old,
P apa's got a cold,
E very day it's really hot,
R unning round in a cold pot,
A te yucky things from a cot,
T oo, too hot,
E very day it's too hot or too cold.

Laura McCrindle (10)
Seafield Primary School, Elgin

RACISM

Racism is bad
Racism is cruel
Racism is evil
And stupid too!

Racism is dull
Racism is daft
Racism is bonkers
And crazy too

Calling names, they think it's a game
But it's not, it fills me with shame.

Joe Kelman (10)
Seafield Primary School, Elgin

RACISM

These harsh words are not a game
To hear racist voices fills me with shame
Don't you show me up with your aggression
People don't want to live with your aggression
Show racism the red card
To treat people with respect is not hard
People shout out and are calling names
Can't they see we are the same?
What sort of person are you?

Kirsty Wilkie (10)
Seafield Primary School, Elgin

ANIMALS

Animals are everywhere,
Most sleep anywhere,
Pups are great!
I want one, I can't wait!

Cats are cool,
They don't drool!
Tigers are sometimes scary,
Big black stripes and very hairy.
Lions are kings of the jungle,
Big cats and very humble.

Snakes some people hate!
Someone was bitten and came to their fate!
Tarantulas are really hairy!
Most people think they're really scary!
Rodents are really cute,
Great big pouches that can scoff the loot!

Cows are big and hairless,
The milk we drink and they're fearless!
Sheep have plain white fleeces,
They're scared of dogs but they're never in pieces.
Oh, animals are so cool
And I am not a fool!

Caitlin Innes (11)
Seafield Primary School, Elgin

DURING THE NIGHT

In the trees wind makes a breeze,
As in the town the sun goes down
And in the street everyone goes to bed,
The street is nearly dead.

In the night I saw wolves fight
And in the trees owls rustle through leaves,
While the Grim Reaper hunts for the dead,
But everyone is still in bed.

As the morning starts to come,
All the children having fun,
While the Grim Reaper goes to Hell
And all his men are unwell!

Garey Steele (11)
Seafield Primary School, Elgin

SHOW RACISM THE RED CARD

These harsh words are not a game
To hear racist voices fills me with shame
Don't be stupid and don't call names
Because we're white
That doesn't matter, let's not fight
Just be nice!

Laura Morrison (10)
Seafield Primary School, Elgin

THE WIND IS EXCITED

The wind is excited
She's whooshing with joy
She's happy because snow is coming to play

The wind is inviting all of her friends
Rain, sleet, lightning and the rest of the gang

She's having a party
The wind is excited
She just can't wait
The wind is whooshing with joy.

Linzi Harvey (11)
Seafield Primary School, Elgin

TOAST TO THE LASSES

We think you're afa nice
We wonder why you're scared a' mice
Some are small, some are big
But whether big or small, we don't give a fig
You come to school with your fancy hair
As if us boys would give a care
Why are you all so loud?
We see you every day and night
But sometimes end up in a fight.

Barrie Thompson (11)
Seafield Primary School, Elgin

Kittens

Cheeky little things
Adorable balls of soft fur
Playful and happy
They caper with their mum
Playing with balls of wool
Feeding when they're hungry
They doze off with mum
But one little kitten is still awake
He still wants to play
But soon his eyes are closing
He joins his brothers and sisters
In dreamland.

Angela Dean (9)
Seafield Primary School, Elgin

The Thunder Is A Loudmouth

The thunder is a loudmouth,
He's like a big car crash,
He speaks to his friend, lightning
And asks what he's doing,
He walks through the clouds,
He hits them if they're in his way,
The thunder is a loudmouth.

Yasmin Anderson (11)
Seafield Primary School, Elgin

The Clouds

The clouds are boring,
Sometimes make shapes,
They're very white and fluffy.

They stop the moon from shining at night,
The shapes sometimes give me a fright.

Chloe Walker (11)
Seafield Primary School, Elgin

The Hurricane Is Mental

He's kicking cars out of his way,
He's throwing houses about,
Running around wrecking everything,
Everybody calls him a bully,
Nobody likes him,
The hurricane is mental.

Jamie Wiseman (11)
Seafield Primary School, Elgin

Shipwreck

In the crystal glass water
There was a ship
A golden galleon
Dead man's skull filled with jewels.

Philip Garioch (12)
Seafield Primary School, Elgin

SUNK

The sea was mad that very night
That ship that sunk that terrible night
As Long John Silver lies below
As golden pearls his eyes we now know
Standing angrily on the bridge
And 700 about
The gloomy ocean I now know.

Ryan O'Shane (11)
Seafield Primary School, Elgin

MY LITTLE SISTER

My little sister is a pest,
She really is the worst,
She really gets on my chest,
I feel I'm really cursed,
But deep down inside my heart,
I wouldn't like us to be apart.

Tanya Ross (11)
Seafield Primary School, Elgin

THE SUN

The sun is very cheeky
As cheeky as can be
She needs to learn some manners
Just like you and me.

Fiona Wilkie (12)
Seafield Primary School, Elgin

THE SNOW IS ANNOYING

The snow is annoying,
He follows you everywhere,
He'll ruin your fun
And spoil your day,
He'll push you over
And he'll do it all day.

So beware,
Because a bully's here;

The snow is annoying,
He follows you everywhere.

Steven Chadwick (11)
Seafield Primary School, Elgin

THE LIGHTNING IS FEROCIOUS

The lightning is ferocious,
He makes his way across the night sky,
Sometimes he hits things,
He kicks down trees,
He knocks over streetlights,
He kicks down walls
And smashes down fences,
He should be locked away,
He fights the thunder,
The lightning is ferocious.

Rebecca Cameron (11)
Seafield Primary School, Elgin

Friends

All my friends are really cool,
Don't worry, they won't pick on you,
They are nice and really funny,
Sometimes their noses are very runny!
Only one out of them all,
Her name is Natalie, she likes to play dolls,
Her hobby is to play mums and dads,
I think she is very sad.

She is my age, I don't know why,
She should be back in Primary 5,
Only joking, she is cool,
She is the leader of the school!

Natasha Macdonald (11)
Seafield Primary School, Elgin

The Snow Is Sad

The snow is sad,
He's always swaying from side to side.

He's never happy,
It would be rare to see him with a smile.

He never talks to anyone,
Not even the wind.

Claire Forbes (11)
Seafield Primary School, Elgin

In The Night

In the night,
I saw some light,
I looked out my window,
The roads were like a ribbon
Of moonlight,
Leaves rustling, cats miaowing,
Shadows dancing, figures prancing,
Moles rooting,
Owls hooting, tree branches waving in the wind,
I have no fear,
Dawn is here.

Cassie McCutcheon (11)
Seafield Primary School, Elgin

Night-Time

In the dead of the night,
When it's dark and gloomy,
The owls start hooting,
The bats come out in the eerie dark,
Along with the badgers white and black.

Cats stealing from the bins,
The rustling of leaves,
The shadowy figures,
Shuffling noises from the ground,
Weird noises and movements all around.

Samantha Mathieson (11)
Seafield Primary School, Elgin

The Waves

The sea comes in,
The waves go out,
You can build a sandcastle,
But the sea will come in and wash it away,
Then the sea will go out,
Carrying your sandcastle.

Shells and seaweed will come in with the waves
And some will go out with the waves.

Waves, I think you're wonderful,
You can be big or small.

The sea comes in,
The waves go out,
Ssshh!

Ashley Barnes (10)
Seafield Primary School, Elgin

The Busy Park

Children screaming with joy
The adults chattering all day
The rusty swings moving slowly
Birds singing way up in the tree

The sirens of the fire engines
The rumbling of people falling
Bikes sliding and skidding
Playing in the park all day.

Kirsty Farquhar (10)
Seafield Primary School, Elgin

HAUNTED HOUSE

One day I walked into a haunted house,
With creepy doors
And ghostly roars,
I walked up the noisy stairs
And under them were hungry bears,
I went into a freaky room,
Ah, there was a loud *boom!*
There was a dark figure,
Who made me shiver,
I ran down the spooky stairs,
So I would not dare to go back there.

Beth Little (10)
Seafield Primary School, Elgin

KANGAROO

The kangaroo bounces
The kangaroo pounces
O' kangaroo, why do you jump?
O' kangaroo, who's your chump?
Kangaroo you never grump
Kangaroo you never slump
On the ground you thump
Thump, thump, thump
On the ground you land
And then away you jump
Jump, jump, jump.

Ross Hudson (11)
Seafield Primary School, Elgin

FRIENDS

Friends always comfort me,
Friends are always there for me,
Friends make me laugh
And in maths, they help me draw my graph,
I don't know what I'd do without my friends!

Samantha is funny,
Heather likes to spend her money,
While Natasha tells a story that's not really funny,
I don't know what I'd do without my friends!

Vicki Smedley (11)
Seafield Primary School, Elgin

NIGHT-TIME

It's night-time in the park,
Not a single dog to bark,
The pond is totally still
And there is a slight chill.

All the animals are asleep,
Not even a frog begins to leap.
The pond looks quite deep,
Is that noise a bleep?

Then a small amount of light,
It must be the end of the night.

Hannah Pacey (11)
Seafield Primary School, Elgin

FRIENDS!

To my friends you're always there,
When you have sweets you always share,
We may have fights,
But we do everything together we even fly our kites.

We go together down the town,
You always turn my frown upside-down,
We won a race,
Going at our fastest pace.

We like to read books,
We like guys that have looks,
We like guys that are cool,
But we don't like the boys at school.

To my friends, you're all the best,
Samantha you are a bit of a pest,
Vicki is quiet and has a big bunny,
Natasha is weird but extremely funny,
Natalie is sporty and kind
And Laura, a better friend I'll never find.
So over all, you are the best!

Heather Penman (11)
Seafield Primary School, Elgin

THE SPIRITS

The spirits are coming
Thump, thump
The spirits are coming
Thump, thump

Everyone is running
Bang, bang
Everyone is running
Bang, bang

Everyone is screaming
Ha, ha
Everyone is screaming
Ha, ha

Everyone is running
Ra, ra
Everyone is running
Ra, ra

The spirits are moving
Pump, pump
The spirits are coming
Boo!

Nathan Mitchell (11)
Seafield Primary School, Elgin

I Smile

I smile when I go ice skating with my family,
I smile when the bell rings at lunchtime.

I smile when I play,
I smile when the class is happy.

I smile when I go to the shop,
I smile when it's Christmas.

I smile when I go on holiday,
I smile when I get a toy.

I smile when I get a bike,
I smile when I fly a kite.

Daniel Clark (9)
Seafield Primary School, Elgin

Football

Football crazy,
Football mad,
We always beat the 6s,
Because we are the lucky lads.

Martin passed to Chilli,
Chilli passed it back,
Martin took a magic shot
And knocked the goalie flat!

Jason Brownless (11)
Seafield Primary School, Elgin

Racism

You are white
I am black
Is it colour that you lack?
Who is coloured
Me or you?

If I were green with envy
If I were red with fury
If I were blue with cold
Then who's coloured
Me or you?

Peta Greer (10)
Seafield Primary School, Elgin

It's Nae A Quinies Game

Quinies think that tha' best at fitba,
Grannies, sisters and yer ma,
Cannae ye tak a hint,
Yer as good as a polo mint.

Fan yer in goals,
Yer as good as a bunch o' moles
And fan will you get ony better,
Until noo if doesna metter.

Lee Stewart (11)
Seafield Primary School, Elgin

Snow

Is snow coming?
It's 10 o'clock,
I keep watching the
Sledges in the garage
And spades too
Everyone's waiting for you
Is snow coming?
It's 12 o'clock,
I keep watching the *tick-tock*
Oh look is that snow
Flying past the window?
Yes it is,
Everyone's having fun
Because morning has begun.

Rhian Fairgrieve (9)
Seafield Primary School, Elgin

The Sea

The sea is like a howling wolf
Splashing on the shore
Fish swimming in its shining waters
Surfers surfing on the waves
Its water filling up the caves
Oh the splash of the sea
Oh the crash of the sea
Oh the sea covering the rocks
The sea fills up the rock pools
So children can use their fishing hooks.

Joshua Bawden (11)
Seafield Primary School, Elgin

SMILE

I smile when I go swimming
I smile when I'm winning

I smile when I go horse riding
I smile when I go gliding

I smile when I go with my dad
I smile when I go mad

I smile when I see my uncle Aaron
I smile when I don't see Darren

I smile when I go on my bike
I smile when I fly my kite.

Stephanie Grieve (9)
Seafield Primary School, Elgin

SEA CREATURE

Looking in the deep blue sea,
A creature was looking back at me,
Big grey eyes, a pointed nose,
Teeth that shone like light bulbs glow.

Skinny fingers, missing toes,
Ears that sprout like flowers grow,
Colours that shine and change with the sun,
The creature's moving and having fun.

Samira Kabbani (10)
Seafield Primary School, Elgin

MY FRIEND

My friend lives in Wales,
Where there are lots of gales,
He lives with his mum and dad,
His mum is lovely but his dad is mad.

My friend is fun,
My friend is jolly,
His favourite treat
Is an ice cream lolly.

He's seen lions in Africa,
He's been to Disney Land in America,
He tried to find Nessie,
Got too near to the edge and ended up all messy.

We talk on the phone both night and day,
I hope one day he'll come and stay,
Here in Scotland he'd feel at home,
Because like in Wales,
We too have lots of gales.

That's the end,
I've got to go,
But before I go,
His name is Joe.

Alastair Milligan (10)
Seafield Primary School, Elgin

BLUE

I like blue,
I think you've guessed,
It's the colour of my team,
Every night when I watch television,
I look for the Premiership.

Yes, I'm a tomboy,
I started playing football,
Now I'm in a team
Called Lossiemouth Ladies.

I've been picked for tons of matches
And my sister as well,
They think we're the stars of the team.

Robbie Porter sponsors us,
Andy Anderson's our main coach,
Rory is who teaches us,
They all like us kids,
We all like them.

This is the team I support, Rangers,
My sister supports Celtic,
So does my brother.

Laura Wilson (10)
Seafield Primary School, Elgin

Purple

Purple here,
Purple there,
Purple, purple,
Everywhere.

Purple, lilac, violet, mauve,
These are colours that I know,
In my room, when I look around,
Everywhere these colours are found.

From duvet to curtains,
From lamps to mats,
My room is completely purple
And that is that.

Purple is my fave colour,
As you've probably guessed,
Even though it may sound nice,
My room's a complete mess!

Jessica Knox (10)
Seafield Primary School, Elgin

My Mum

My mum is fun
She eats hot buns
And she loves her karaoke
I hit her in the face
With a snowball (and in the waist)
And she thought it was very funny.

Leanne Kelly (10)
Seafield Primary School, Elgin

SMILE

I smile when I go to bed at night,
I smile when I am allowed to fly my kite.

I smile when I go to the beach,
I smile when our teacher is ready to teach.

I smile when I do a jigsaw puzzle,
I smile when I get a cuddle.

I smile when people are nice,
I smile when my dad makes rice.

I smile when I go to school,
I smile when I go to the pool.

I smile when I play with my mum,
I smile when I eat a hot cross bun.

Lucy McShane (9)
Seafield Primary School, Elgin

FOOTBALL

I like playing football,
Especially at school,
My favourite team is Rangers
I think they're really cool.

When I go to Ibrox,
To see my heroes play,
And when I see them score a goal,
I shout, 'Hip hip hooray!'

Scott McKee (10)
Seafield Primary School, Elgin

The Wee Black Dog

There was a wee black dog called Sparkle
Out for a walk one day
She was running, jumping and barking
And chasing the birds for play
The birds she was chasing were seagulls
Because she was down by the sea
But she couldn't catch up because she couldn't fly
And she was also very wee!
She ran to the left and ran to the right
And got in a muddle
She took a leap into the air
And landed in what she thought was a puddle!
Well she splashed and she spluttered
All for a whim!
But she never forgot
It was her first swim!

Charlie Welsh (9)
Seafield Primary School, Elgin

Bull

Bull, bull, it is just a fool,
Rage, red, fat and with a big head,
Ramming like a wrestler with a smelly belly
Like Ally Anderson,
But the bull has a big hammer
And he is coming after you now.

Dean Webster (10)
Seafield Primary School, Elgin

SMILE

I smile when my pets are happy,
I smile when my budgie isn't yappy.

I smile when I go swimming,
I smile when my dad isn't singing.

I smile when the bell rings at 3.15,
I smile when my shoes have a nice sheen.

I smile when the weekend is here,
I smile when the future is clear.

I smile when it is sunny,
I smile when I eat honey.

I smile when it is snowing,
I smile when I know where I am going.

I smile when Christmas is here,
I smile when I hear people cheer.

Lauren Wimble (9)
Seafield Primary School, Elgin

SCHOOL

School is boring
School is glum
I wish I could tell my mum
I wish I was home
Home is fab
I never want to go to school
School is *bad!*

Grant Fletcher (10)
Seafield Primary School, Elgin

SMILE

I smile when I do experiments,
I smile when my mum gives me peppermints.

I smile when I eat fruit,
I smile when I eat my granny's soup.

I smile when I do PE,
I smile when I watch Takeshi's Castle on TV.

I smile when I have fun,
I smile when I make buns.

I smile when I see ducks,
I smile when I hear chickens go *cluck.*

I smile when I go on holiday,
I smile when people help other people who are in poverty.

I smile when I go to the zoo,
I smile when my dog comes too!

Demi Tewnion (9)
Seafield Primary School, Elgin

SNOWING

It snowed all day
And snowed all night
I went out to play
All crunchy and white

No school
Wahoo! Let's go
And build a snowman
And go sledging down the hill.

Jamie Neil (10)
Seafield Primary School, Elgin

SMILE

I smile when I skate,
I smile when I paint.

I smile when I eat a banana,
I smile when I see my nana.

I smile when I go riding,
I smile when I go sliding.

I smile when I go to school,
I smile when I go to the swimming pool.

I smile when I see my uncle Barry and Liz,
I smile when I do a quiz.

I smile when I go on holiday with my family,
I smile when my friends play happily.

I smile when I see my mum,
I smile when I eat a bun.

Christina Marshall (9)
Seafield Primary School, Elgin

GRANNY AND GRANDAD SCOTT

My granny likes to dance
She also smells like flowers
When she goes into a shop
She can be there for hours

My grandad likes to play golf
He also likes to watch telly
When I go to visit him
He feeds me lots of jelly.

Josie Scott (9)
Seafield Primary School, Elgin

When I Smile

I smile when I arrive at school,
I smile when I go to the pool.

I smile when my brother gives me money,
I smile when my mum gave me a bunny.

I smile when I paint,
I smile when I faint.

I smile when my birthday comes,
I smile when my dad plays the drums.

I smile when I play with my friends,
I smile when the weekend ends.

I smile when I smell cakes baking,
I smile when my brother's tooth's aching.

I smile when I do the Highland Fling,
I smile when I sing.

Chantelle Ord (9)
Seafield Primary School, Elgin

Summer

The sun's been shining
For days and days
Making everything hot
With its golden rays

The river got so hot
The water went away
Now Sam and Pam
Can't go fishing today.

Sarah Watts (9)
Seafield Primary School, Elgin

The Weather

The weather in Scotland is different
To the weather in England and Wales,
In Wiltshire we had gentle breezes
But up here we have really strong gales.

In Scotland we've just had some white stuff,
A blanket of snow on the ground,
People were sledging and throwing snowballs
And building snowmen all around.

Last year with the rain Elgin flooded
And people were washed from their homes.
Don't think this has happened in Swindon,
Some folk even lost all their gnomes!

Last summer was lovely and sunny,
It really was warm in the south,
So fingers crossed for some sunshine this year,
For the folk living near Lossiemouth.

Chloe Baxter (8)
Seafield Primary School, Elgin

I Smile

I smile when I see Mrs Smith,
I smile when I have a lift.

I smile when the bells ring,
I smile when my sister goes *ding-aling-aling*.

I smile when I play with Logan and Molly,
I smile when I have a lolly.

I smile when I get new clothes,
I smile when I smell a rose.

Taran Read (9)
Seafield Primary School, Elgin

Smile

I smile when the bell rings at 3.15
I smile when I watch Mr Bean

I smile when I go to the pool
I smile when it is the end of school

I smile when I watch TV
I smile when I play with my friend, Lee

I smile when I stay in bed
I smile when I have a heavy head

I smile when I complete my work
I smile when I am covered in dirt

I smile when I eat a cake
I smile when I go fishing at the lake

I smile when a dog can bark
I smile when I go to the Cooper Park

I smile when I play football
I smile when I go to the town hall

I smile when I cook with my mum
I smile when I play my drum

I smile when I am happy
I smile when my brother isn't yappy

I smile when I go to the beach
I smile when I eat a peach

I smile when I ride a bike
I smile when I fly a kite

I smile when I am not awake
I smile when I draw a shape

I smile when I see a whale
I smile when I go to a sale

I smile when I play a game
I smile when my photo is in a frame

I smile when I play with a spade
I smile when my model is made

I smile when I see my dad
I smile when he calls me lad.

Calum Davies (9)
Seafield Primary School, Elgin

SMILING

I smile when I am me,
I smile when I am free.

I smile when I am invited to parties,
I smile when I eat Smarties.

I smile when I go home from school,
I smile when my stepdad plays pool.

I smile when my granny and grandpa come down,
I smile when I go down town.

I smile when I get a treat,
I smile when I get a lucky seat.

I smile when I get a new pet,
I smile when I get a new make-up set.

I smile when I play with my friends,
I smile when I play with my friends at weekends.

I smile when I go down to the lake,
I smile when I get my birthday cake.

Joanna O'Neill (9)
Seafield Primary School, Elgin

I Smile

I smile when I get my way
I smile when it's a rainy day

I smile when my family are happy
I smile when I am yappy

I smile when I go to school
I smile when I am a fool

I smile when I am right
I smile when I am out of sight

I smile when the bell goes
I smile when I sell some clothes

I smile when I go to bed
I smile when I bang my head

I smile when I watch the telly
I smile when I feed my belly

I smile when I go for a walk
I smile when I talk and talk

I smile when it is sunny
I smile when I eat honey

I smile when I get some money
I smile when I am funny

I smile when I get a teddy
I smile when tea is ready.

Lucy Redfern (9)
Seafield Primary School, Elgin

Smile

I smile when I get my own way,
I smile when it is a sunny day.

I smile when I get money,
I smile when people are funny.

I smile when I make a cake,
I smile when I eat a flake.

I smile when there is sand,
I smile when there is a band.

I smile when I play a game,
I smile when people say my name.

I smile when I make a shape,
I smile when I bake chocolate cake.

I smile when I have a bath,
I smile when I laugh.

Kieran Butcher (8)
Seafield Primary School, Elgin

Things I Like

I like to go swimming,
I like to go to my bed.

I like to go to school with my friends,
I like to go on my bike.

I like to go to the park,
I like to go to my gran's.

I like to go to the discos,
I like to go to the parties.

Sam Sherwin (9)
Seafield Primary School, Elgin

I Smile

I smile when Christmas comes,
I smile when I have fun.

I smile when my dad becomes dumb,
I smile when I get to play with everyone.

I smile when my mum becomes cool,
I smile when I have fun in the pool.

I smile when I read a book,
I smile when I try to cook.

I smile when I smell a flower,
I smile when I take a hot shower.

I smile when I have good dreams,
I smile when I eat an ice cream.

I smile when I am happy,
I smile when my brother isn't yappy.

Kaylie McRae (9)
Seafield Primary School, Elgin

Smiling

I smile when I get new toys,
I smile when I get home to no noise.

I smile when I go on my holiday,
I smile when I play with my friends.

I smile when I tell the truth,
I smile when I give people presents.

I smile when I see people donate blood,
I smile when I go swimming.

Andrew McKenzie (9)
Seafield Primary School, Elgin

Smile On My Face

I smile when I go swimming
I smile when I am winning

I smile when I go on holiday
I smile when I go to Spey Bay

I smile when I play in the snow
I smile when I see my friend, Joe

I smile when Stephanie plays with me
I smile when I have my tea

I smile when I talk to my mum
I smile when I get taught a sum

I smile when there is a new family member
I smile when it is December

I smile when I go for a ride
I smile when my friends are by my side.

Megan McQueen (8)
Seafield Primary School, Elgin

Smiling

I smile when I'm on my bike
I smile because it's the best toy I like

I smile when I go swimming with my friends
I smile when I play with them

I smile when I go on holiday
I smile when I get there

I smile when I go to the park
I smile when I go on the swings.

Scott McGarrie (9)
Seafield Primary School, Elgin

Some Things That I Adore

I really, really love my cat,
So cuddly and so very fat,
I just can't put her down,
I would hate it if she were to drown.

I adore the way she purrs,
I laugh when she miaows.

Pipkin is an unusual name,
Maybe someday she will be in a hall of fame.

Sometime she will die,
Then I will begin to cry.

Dear, dear, oh pussy cat, now you're dead,
I can't bear to go to bed.

Your little grave reminds me of how we used to play,
That really was a great, great day.

But now you're gone and we're alone in separate worlds,
I miss you pussy cat.

David Manson (9)
Seafield Primary School, Elgin

Smile

I smile when it's my birthday
I smile when I play the PlayStation 2
I smile when I go swimming
I smile when I go on holiday with my family
I smile when school ends
I smile when I fly a kite
I smile when I have a bath.

Steven Curran (9)
Seafield Primary School, Elgin

Shyness Is . . .

Shyness is the redness,
Creeping up my face.

Shyness is meeting new people,
In a brand new place.

Shyness is feeling silly,
When people look at you.

Shyness is feeling scared,
You don't know what to do.

Shyness is so strange,
You're annoyed but you feel the tears.

Shyness is very frightening,
But you have to face your fears.

Shyness is a feeling of complete and utter hell,
But why do we feel so bad when others feel it as well?

Laura Penny (12)
Slains Primary School, Ellon

MY BEST FRIEND

My best friend is Laura Penny,
She is there when you are down,
Always smiling, never a frown,
She is the best at Tae Kwon-Do
Definitely the best that I know.

I like Laura because she makes me laugh,
Sometimes she is very daft,
I have been to her house lots of times,
We made this drink that was very fine.

We both think school is very boring,
Once in P4 she was almost snoring,
I also like her because she is fun,
We play outside in the sun.

Zoe Sinclair (10)
Slains Primary School, Ellon

FIREWORKS

Fireworks are very bright,
Once you have set them alight.
They are blue, yellow and red,
But not the colour of lead.
I like rockets,
But don't put them in your pockets.
I've always had a desire,
To have a bonfire.
Keep your pets inside,
And let them hide.
Little children might get a fright,
On a dark Bonfire Night.

Lisa M Irvine (12)
Westhill Primary School, Westhill

My Cousin

My baby cousin Rachel
Only two and three quarters
Really is the best
She has a small ponytail at the back of her head
She is really cute and cuddly
She likes the Teletubbies
But she loves The Tweenies the best
She slobbers everywhere!
She has a cool playroom
Full of games and toys
(When I don't do what she says
She pushes me around)
Apart from that, I love her
All the rest of the time.

Jamie McNaughton (11)
Westhill Primary School, Westhill

My Best Friend, Kayleigh

Kayleigh is my best mate,
She is as cool as Avril Lavigne.
Kayleigh is a creamy cup of hot chocolate,
She is a tub of triple chocolate ice cream that everyone loves,
She is as talkative as a buzzing alarm clock.
Kayleigh is a magical sunset with every colour in the world,
I've got 100s of nicknames for her but *Dude McDee* is my favourite,
She has got long thick creamy brown hair,
She is as artistic as Picasso,
She is the best friend I could ever ask for.

Emily Pettitt (11)
Westhill Primary School, Westhill

Memories

Inside my head are a million memories . . .

Going to Cyprus
Having an eye operation
When my hamster died
Winning the player of the year award
Losing my Santa toy in Manchester Airport

Going for trials with Aberdeen Select
Getting an ear infection on holiday
Getting a new hamster
When we beat Aberdeen Lads club 15-0
Being chosen for the school football team
Getting to the final of the Westhill Gala
Going on a camel ride.

Harry Burness (11)
Westhill Primary School, Westhill

My Grandad

My grandad is funny because he can swear for Scotland
And talk gibberish for England
And he always talks about when he was in the jungle!
He always talks about where he has been
Historical landmarks and what he likes to eat
He doesn't really like football
And likes the colour green
Whenever Aberdeen loses he is the first to say they're rubbish
But when they win he says 'Wasn't it a good game?'

Lewis Illingworth (11)
Westhill Primary School, Westhill

My Memories

Inside my head are a million memories . . .

Swimming with Greek turtles,
Getting on my first aeroplane,
Being in plaster from my toe to my thigh
For my 2nd birthday,
Getting a new puppy,
Going on holiday with my best friend to Centre Parks in Bristol,
Getting metal wire screws and a metal plate put in my arm,
Seeing a lightning storm in Greece,
Seeing my newborn baby cousin
Being in plaster for all my even numbered birthdays except one,
Touching a sea cucumber,
Swimming with hundreds of starfish,
Being scared out of my mind by a living statue,
Going to Buckingham Palace.

Emma Rae (11)
Westhill Primary School, Westhill

My Cool Dad!

My dad was brave to stand up
In a fairy dress,
We were in Cyprus but you wouldn't have guessed!
There were people dressed as taxi drivers
Who thought they were in Inverness,
While at the party I got stuck in the lift
After I gave a gift.

Aidan Fleming (11)
Westhill Primary School, Westhill

Tilly

She came from Tyrebagger
Two sisters and two brothers.
She's a cocker spaniel,
(I'd say a cocker spaniel cross-mountain goat.)
She's mad!
When she runs, her ears flop up and down.
(She's fast!)
She likes to play pounce and chase.
She's got nicknames Waucester Sauce and Tillywoglpops.
Tilly loves to have cuddles,
Her best friends are Logan and Budge.
She loves toast and chicken.
Tilly's a chocolate roan,
My best friend!

Victoria Willan (10)
Westhill Primary School, Westhill

Baby Carley

My cutest friend, Carley is the *best* of them all!
She always makes me laugh.
She has her milk bottle and always blows it out!
She watches Saturday morning shows
And dances round and round!
She does raspberries at you and looks at you as if you're daft!
She has got dark hair with her little mini ears pierced!
She wears a big puffy dress when she's going out.
She sleeps with her mum and dad
And wears her Winnie the Pooh suit!
I will never forget her
And she will always be my friend!

Kelsey Longmuir (11)
Westhill Primary School, Westhill

My Granda

My granda is the coolest,
He plays PlayStation games,
But when he fails a level,
He starts to shout out names!
He's always on the PlayStation
When I want a go,
So he asks me how to switch it off,
Because he doesn't know.

Apart from playing PlayStation games,
He likes to watch TV,
Countdown is his favourite,
But it really bores me!

He forgets to take his tablets,
Before and after tea,
He says I should have reminded him,
But he never asks me!

Steven Repper (11)
Westhill Primary School, Westhill

Blue

Blue is the calm, Caribbean sea.
Blue is the colour of sadness and loneliness.
Blue is the sky-diving chameleon.
Blue is a dazzling waterfall.
Blue is the colour of a summer sky.
Blue is mysterious and magical.
Blue is a marine on parade.
Blue is Pluto, a dot in the faraway distance.

Callum Ogston (11) & Ewan Mackay (12)
Westhill Primary School, Westhill

My Granny And Grandad

My grandad is the coolest,
He helps me with my maths.
He has a strange sense of humour,
But he always makes me laugh.

My granny is the funniest,
She likes to go on rides
That go in all directions,
But my grandad runs and hides.

My grandad is the strangest,
He's really in to pop.
Like Steps and S Club 7,
Garage and hip-hop.

My granny is the funkiest,
She does housework all the time,
I would really hate it
If that job was mine.

I love my granny and grandad,
They're special you can see,
There's a place in my heart
Where they will always be.

Jenna Goff (11)
Westhill Primary School, Westhill

My Cats

I have two pets, they are both cats,
but sometimes they think they're acrobats.

They are a mixture of colour,
one is orange, the other's black.
They don't seem to mind that much,
but they're still very *fat!*

They're really, really cute,
their names are Sooty and Ginger.
But when Sooty gets told off,
she is a bit of a whinger.

Even though Ginger's a real nice cat,
when it's raining outside,
he does his business on the bathroom mat!

Even though they can be naughty
and sometimes just plain bad,
they are still the best cats in the whole wide world,
the best I've ever had.

Michael MacDonald (11)
Westhill Primary School, Westhill

MISTY

Misty was my pony,
She loved to jump, eat and sleep.
She would canter up and down the hill,
Then stop and rub herself on the fence and rip her rug.
She could jump huge fences from a standstill,
When we raced my mum up the field, we always won!
Her best horsey friend was Kelly and human friend – me!
We had gone through millions of rugs because she always ripped them.
If I took her for show jumping, no one would stand a chance,
Her show name was Frosted Doughnut,
I always bought her the best presents.
She could run in the Grand National and win.
She would win cross country with her eyes closed, going backwards.
Misty was the best pony anyone could have,
But sadly this fab pony passed away.

Ailsa Mullins (11)
Westhill Primary School, Westhill

FEAR IS . . .

Fear is a madman coming straight at you,
Fear is bombs hidden in your house,
Fear is something knocking on your window,
Fear is instant death awaiting,
Fear is being lost in the middle of nowhere,
Fear is spirits coming to haunt you,
Fear is bills piling in,
Fear is doing something stupid in front of a crowd,
Fear is a creaky door opening,
Fear is sharks gobbling you up,
Fear is the big black thing from under the bed,
Fear is fear!

Euan Dodds (9)
Westhill Primary School, Westhill

Fear Is . . .

Fear is when you're in the shower and your sister switches the light off.
Fear is when you're in your bed and you hear a creak.
Fear is when you lose your parents in town.
Fear is when you forget to do your homework.
Fear is that one day I'll die.
Fear is going to a new school.
Fear is that there might be World War 3.
Fear is going on a boat.
Fear is Michael Jackson.
Fear is not finishing my work.
Fear is getting into trouble.
Fear is scary.

Scott Milne (9)
Westhill Primary School, Westhill

My Grandfather's Cat

My grandfather's cat is quiet,
She tiptoes like a mouse.
She is sly and sneaky.
Her name is Snowy,
Though I think she should be called Speedy.
Snowy hides behind a bush,
Then when she sees a bird,
She moves in for the kill.
Snowy then delicately moves fast but slyly,
Then catches the oblivious bird!
Yet she can be gentle, soft and soulfully caring,
I know she is not mine, but I couldn't love her more!

Katie Jones (11)
Westhill Primary School, Westhill

Happiness Is . . .

Happiness is when you have just found out you have won £20.
Happiness is when you find out that Christmas is two days away.
Happiness is when you find out that you have won a family holiday.
Happiness is when you find out that you are allowed to go and
see the film you wanted to see.
Happiness is that you have a family.
Happiness is that you have a best friend.
Happiness is that you have lots of money.
Happiness is that you can have lots of toys.
Happiness is that you are not bored.
Happiness is that you are special.
Happiness is that you are a good person.
Happiness is that you are the best.

Johanna Goldie (9)
Westhill Primary School, Westhill

Memories

Inside my head are a million memories . . .
Getting four teeth out
Losing my Gameboy Advance on a plane
My 10th birthday
Going into Primary 1
Aberdeen beating Celtic 2-0
Scoring my first goal from defence
Going to my first swimming gala
My first school trip
Going to Canada
The smell of Shaws sweet factory
Getting my dog
Christmas Day
First football match winning 18-0!

Michael Ridley (11)
Westhill Primary School, Westhill

My Little Cousin Emma

My little cousin Emma has just turned one,
She is so cute and crawls all the time.

With all her toys and very cute clothes,
She is a cuddly bundle of joy.

She loves her dolly Madge,
But just as much as her other one Holly.

My auntie takes her out for walks,
She loves them and normally falls asleep.

When she's settled in her bed,
You normally don't hear a peep.

I love my baby cousin and I always will,
Even when she grows up to be as big as me!

Morag Will (11)
Westhill Primary School, Westhill

Red

Red is an angry teacher
Red is the sky at night
Red is the flame of a burning match
Red is a big juicy wart
Red is Mars soaring in space
Red is Man United's strip
Red is Santa's suit
Red is Rudolph's nose
Red is a cricket ball
Red is a fire engine
Red is a burnt man's head.

Fraser Clarke & David Sutherland (11)
Westhill Primary School, Westhill

My Best Friend

My best friend is a warm glowing sunset
She has a loud laugh
She is a creamy heart full of mallow
She has a head full of fibs
She has a sweet smelling flower in her hair
She could wiggle her bum out of trouble
She could talk for Scotland
She can breathe through her ears
She is a rainbow full of colours
She is a model with her high heels
She is a sherbet lemon just waiting to explode
She is a prim, beautiful princess
She is a cool, trendy fashion icon - admired by all
She is a soft scoop of ice cream waiting to melt
She is the best friend in the whole wide world
- What more could I ask for?

Kayleigh Milne (11)
Westhill Primary School, Westhill

Red

Red is thick blood
Red is tomato sauce being squeezed from the bottle
Red is a romantic rose
Red is steaming hot magma
Red is a throbbing human heart
Red is the flaming tips of a fire
Red is the colour of a speeding Ferrari.

Arron Sturrock & Oran Lasocki (11)
Westhill Primary School, Westhill